PRAISE for RAISING BOOKWORMS

"Raising Bookworms does something rare—it recognizes that to get a kid reading means lighting an internal fire, not just applying an external push. This book shows you how to make reading a habit they'll want to form all on their own."

James Patterson, Multi-Bestselling Author,
19 Consecutive #1 titles; NY Times Adult and
Children's #1 bestseller list simultaneously

"If children did come with a parenting manual, this would be it. Good books are the core of good parenting, and *Raising Bookworms* is a common-sense guide to instilling a love of reading in your children. Given the right guidance and incentives, children will read for the sheer joy of it. This practical guide to how to make that connection is an essential resource for every parent and parent to be.

Lovingly written and packed with recommended reading and activities for parents and children, this essential guide to raising readers connects children with the joy of discovering the world through books. The message is simple: Children can learn to love reading books. Caring attentive adults can make the difference, and that difference changes lives."

—Leonard Kniffel, Editor in Chief
American Libraries

"Emma Walton Hamilton's *Raising Bookworms* celebrates the experience of bonding with children through books and shows just how dynamic and creative a process that can be. Reading aloud, dramatizing stories, and using books as guides to the arts, sciences and larger world, are just a few of the great ideas shared here. Raising Bookworms is filled with tips for parents and caregivers of children of all ages, and it reminds us of the joys and benefits of having books as part of our lives."

—**Susan Raab,** children's literature industry consultant
Raab Associates Inc.

"Parents who bemoan the fact that their children cannot read, do not read for pleasure, or spend too much time watching television or playing on the computer can turn to the well organized and informative *Raising Bookworms* by Emma Walton Hamilton—a blueprint for building successful readers. *Raising Bookworms* excels in suggesting ideas for scenarios that encourage reading. Many parents hesitate to read to their children because they feel uncomfortable reading aloud. Using her theatrical background, Ms. Hamilton makes simple suggestions that would assist any shy parent. Those who turn to this book will learn how to make their home into a reading studio that will catapult their little ones into a life of literary success."

—**Ilene Abramson,** Director of Children's Services
Los Angeles Public Library

"The book is filled with words of wisdom and inspiration, but the practical tips will help parents ensure that their children not only can read but love to read. The tables at the end offer a tidy matrix of activities that will reinforce reading efforts."

—**Jeanette Larson,** Children's Literature Consultant
TLA "Librarian of the Year," Austin, TX

"I think *Raising Bookworms* should be required reading for all parents of school-aged children and for all educators. If more people found joy in life, the world would be a better place. Joy in reading would open so many doors for each child. It's the springboard to a lifetime of success."

—Jennie Dunham, Children's Literature Agent
Dunham Literary

"Emma Walton Hamilton's many practical, thoughtful, sensible, creative, kid-friendly, and just plain fun strategies for raising bookworms are just what all parents need to get their children reading and loving it. Her annotated booklists of family favorites for preschool through middle school underscore her simplest and most important hypothesis: Reading=JOY. What better gift can we give our children?"

—Judy Freeman, Children's Literature Consultant,
Author of *Books Kids Will Sit Still For*

"Stories make us human, and reading them connects children with a multitude of worlds and possibilities. Emma Walton Hamilton knows this, and has brought stories to life in her work in the theater and in her books for children. Now, in *Raising Bookworms*, she gives the rest of us the tools we need to share stories with the children we love. A clear, concise, and hands-on manual for parents, educators, and anyone interested in celebrating the written word."

—Catherine Creedon, librarian and author
Blue Wolf

"Emma Walton Hamilton has the key to putting joy back into reading for children. Her tips and suggestions for reading together as a family activity are a boon to busy parents and will lead them to many happy connections with their children."

—**Connie C. Rockman,** Children's Literature Consultant
Author/Editor of *Book of Junior Authors
and Illustrators* (Editions 8, 9 & 10)

"*Raising Bookworms* is the book that every family needs! It is filled with brilliant and creative ways to bring the pure pleasure of reading into your child's life—a gift that if given early will stay with them forever. As a family that spends all of their time together making music—reading together is still such an important part of our lives. Thank you, Emma, for sharing what we believe to be one of the greatest gifts of all."

—**Lisa Michaelis, and Billy and Emily Schlosser,**
"Laughing Pizza"

Raising Bookworms

Getting Kids Reading for Pleasure and Empowerment

Emma Walton Hamilton

beech
tree
books

BEECH TREE BOOKS

www.beechtreebooks.com

Publisher's Cataloging in Publication

Hamilton, Emma Walton.
  Raising bookworms: getting kids reading for pleasure and empowerment / by Emma Walton Hamilton.
    p. cm.
  Includes bibliographical references.
  LCCN 2008902969
  ISBN-13 978-0-9815833-0-3
  ISBN-10 0-9815833-0-X

  1. Reading—Parent participation. 2. Children—Books and reading. 3. Reading.

LB1050.H36 2009   372.41

Cover design by Annemarie McCoy – www.barkingfish.biz
Book layout by Shawn Morningstar and Marian Hartsough Associates

Quantity discounts are available for special promotions and premiums, including corporate and educational programs, subscription incentives, gifts or fundraising campaigns

For more information please contact the publisher at:

BEECH TREE BOOKS
PO Box 839,
Sag Harbor, NY 11963
888-631-3393
mail@beechtreebooks.com
www.beechtreebooks.com

Printed on recycled paper

For Steve, Sam and Hope,
who redefine joy for me every day.

"A child has no great wish to perfect himself in the use of an instrument of torture, but make it a means to his pleasure, and soon you will not be able to keep him from it."

—Daniel Pennac, author & educator, *Better Than Life*

Acknowledgments

This book would not have been possible without the generosity and help of a number of people.

Heartfelt thanks to those trusted friends and advisors who took the time to read the manuscript and provide me with invaluable feedback and support, including: Ilene Abramson, GraceAnne DeCandido, Jennie Dunham, Judy Freeman, Nick Glass, Leonard Kniffel, Jeanette Larson, James Patterson, Susan Raab, Connie Rockman, Maria Salvadore, Lisa Michaelis and Billy and Emily Schlosser, and Clarissa Wilder. Additional thanks to Cathy Creedon, who not only read the manuscript and shared her thoughts and recommendations, but helped me with cataloguing information as well.

To my longtime friend and colleague, Eliza Rand, thank you for the constant encouragement, enthusiasm, ideas, research and belly laughs. And to web guru and pal Annemarie McCoy, thank you for the jacket art, web wizardry and hours of online fun.

Dana Melichar, Alice Smith, Vicky Dominski and Cheryl Nordt—thank you for making it possible for me to put in the necessary hours! (Extra thanks to Dana for research assistance.)

Special thanks to Peter Bowerman for providing mentorship throughout the process, and for making everything seem clear and manageable. On the technical end, thanks to my super editor "down under" Geoff Whyte, as well as to Shawn Morningstar and Marian Hartsough for terrific typesetting and endless patience, Cathleen Small and Katherine Stimson for ace proofreading and indexing, respectively, Ceil Frank and Michael Yurick at Ocean Printing, and Shelly Sapyta and the terrific team at Bookmasters/AtlasBooks.

The enduring faith, generosity and creativity of Susan, Joyce and the family at Raab Associates continue to be a huge gift to me, as does the bounteous wisdom and guidance of Libbe HaLevy. I am also deeply grateful to Steve Sauer, for his contribution these past years toward making my writing and editing dreams come true.

Both sets of my wonderful, creative parents raised me to be a book-worm, and for that, as well as for their enduring love and encouragement, I thank them from the bottom of my heart.

Finally, my everlasting love and gratitude to Steve, Sam, and Hope for their unlimited patience and support while Mom hammered away at the keys. You are my inspiration.

Thank you *all!*

Table of Contents

I

Introduction

"Half of the American people have never read a newspaper. Half have never voted for President. One hopes it is the same half."

—Gore Vidal, author

"How can I get my child to turn off the TV (computer, Gameboy, cell phone, etc.) and pick up a *book*?"

As a professional educator, children's book author and editor, this is the question I hear most often—a near-constant lament at virtually every public appearance, speaking engagement, book signing, or school program I do. In fact, according to a recent survey by Scholastic, eighty-two percent of parents say they wish their child would read more books for fun. And I understand, because as a parent, I've felt this way myself, and I'm guessing that most likely you have, too.

In fact, since you've picked up this book, I feel fairly safe in making a few assumptions about you.

You've probably read a newspaper or two—maybe on a regular basis. And you're probably interested in children, maybe even totally dedicated to a special one or two or more. I'd even go so far as to guess that you're already convinced of the value of reading . . . although perhaps somewhat perplexed as to how to help your children, or children in general, to share your enthusiasm.

You're likely well aware of the fact that children who read well do better in other subjects, and in *all* aspects of life, both at school and beyond. And you may even know that readers are twice as likely to attend performing arts events, visit museums, attend sporting events, do volunteer or charity work, and *vote* than their non-reading counterparts.

Chances are, you already believe, as I do, that there's a direct relationship between reading skills and our ability to participate in the world with confidence as an informed citizen, able to communicate effectively, succeed in our chosen career, enjoy rewarding relationships, and achieve personal fulfillment.

The bad news is, in spite of the compelling benefits outlined above, a recent survey by the National Endowment for the Arts based on more than two decades of census reports states that, for the first time in modern history, *less than half the adult [American] population now reads literature for pleasure.*

This decline in reading has occurred irrespective of age, gender, or race, and is most pronounced among the young.

Here are some perhaps lesser-known, but definitely more disturbing, facts[1]:

- Fifty percent of American adults are unable to read an eighth-grade-level book.

- More than twenty percent of adults read at or below a fifth-grade level—way below the level needed to earn a living wage.

- Children who haven't developed some basic literacy skills by the time they enter school are three to four times more likely to drop out in later years.

- It is estimated that illiteracy costs businesses and taxpayers $20 billion each year.

- Forty-two percent of college graduates never read another book once they have graduated.

---

[1]Sources: *Illiterate America*, Jonathan Kozol; National Center for Adult Literacy/US Dept. of Education; National Center for Education Statistics; National Institute for Literacy; www.bookstatistics.com; United Way.

- Eighty percent of U.S. families did not buy or read a book last year.
- Seventy percent of U.S. adults have not been in a bookstore in the last five years.

Truth is, America now ranks a distant last among eighteen nations with respect to literacy levels for high school graduates between the ages of sixteen and twenty-five, with fifty-nine percent in this age group considered "functionally illiterate." That figure is eighteen percent lower than in Poland, the country with the second lowest level of literacy.

America's founders, living as they did in an age when the printed word was the primary means of communication, placed a high emphasis on protecting the "marketplace of ideas" so that public discourse could flourish. Today, that discourse is predominantly one-way—we "receive" information from our television sets, radios, computers, and iPods. Large media corporations pay vast sums of money to explore new ways in which we can be collectively massaged toward a certain purchase or perspective. And the more we sit and stare at the screen, the more we turn our back on the kind of thoughtful reasoning that interaction with the written word promotes . . . and, the more mute we become.

What's the Answer—And What Qualifies Me to Suggest It?

Let me be very up front here. While I am an arts educator, I am not a trained reading specialist, nor do I have a teaching degree. This book does not attempt to address the global, cultural, or socioeconomic aspects of literacy, nor will it address the *mechanics* of reading. These issues are best addressed by economists, sociologists, literacy experts, and reading specialists, to whose collective wisdom and dedication I'm happy to defer.

What I *am* is the co-author of sixteen books for children, an arts education administrator, a teaching artist, and a passionate advocate for literacy and the arts. I've spent literally hundreds of hours reading to, and with, young people in classrooms, libraries, and other venues across the country, and have created and managed unique performance and arts education programs for young audiences for more than fifteen years. I've developed writing curriculums and teachers' guides, and have taught hundreds of high and middle school students the tools of dramatic writing and the value of arts appreciation. As a professional editor, I've shepherded dozens of children's books by other authors through the publication process.

I'm also a passionate reader, and have repeatedly turned to books over and over again throughout my life, and continue to do so, for pleasure, knowledge, solace, and empowerment. My particular penchant for nonfiction—be it biographies, histories, or motivational/educational books—has taught me the skills I've needed over the years to become a better parent, wife, teacher, producer, director, writer, editor, money manager, traveler, homemaker, gardener, organizer . . . the list goes on and on.

Perhaps most importantly, I'm the mother of two children—a daughter in preschool and a son in middle school—both of whom love to read.

My experience with children, both my own and those with whom I work in arts education programs and through my publishing work, has brought me to a fundamental conclusion: *Success in any creative endeavor—including reading—is most often achieved when that activity is associated with pleasure.*

Seems obvious, right? Actually, this critically important connection is often overlooked, forgotten, or just plain abandoned by parents and educators alike in favor of other—mostly academic—ambitions and objectives.

What You Will Find in These Pages

This book is about creating—or restoring—the connection between reading and joy. It's about providing young people with the tools and the appetite to continue to seek out reading for their own gratification and growth in later life.

The strategies are laid out according to age groupings, from birth through early adolescence. Some span all ages, while others are unique to a particular age group or have been modified for each level. You may choose to read only those sections that apply to your particular child or children's age group, however bear in mind that children develop at different rates and have different makeups, therefore many of the strategies will be equally applicable and effective across the various age groups. At the risk of repeating some information, I have included a brief recap of all previously outlined suggestions in each subsequent section, along with a note of the page numbers on which the detailed information can be found. There are also review tables encompassing all the ideas and recommendations located in the appendix.

I'm a great believer in the synergies that exist between literacy and the arts—and the ways in which each can inform and support the other—so you will find many of the activities in these pages stemming from that orientation. I have also included practical, kinesthetic suggestions for simple environmental cues and non-verbal messages that support the association of reading with joyful experiences.

"In the highest civilization, the book is still the highest delight. He who has once known its satisfactions is provided with a resource against calamity."

—Ralph Waldo Emerson

Finally, there are dozens of recommendations for age-appropriate book selections, as well as other resources to further the cause. These lists are by no means comprehensive, for there are many other wonderful books, ideas, and strategies, but limitations of space preclude me from covering them all. They are, however, a reflection of what has worked for us as a family—books and techniques that have stood the test of time, and that I can share with confidence and an open heart. By all means, turn to your own favorites first when making reading selections for your children, and please don't infer that if a favorite of yours is not included in any of my lists, it is a deliberate omission.

For ongoing updates to these lists, visit www.raisingbookworms.com. And, I would love to hear about your *own* strategies for getting kids reading—and loving it—for future editions of, or sequels to, this book.

A Vision for the Future

It's abundantly clear that the digital age has radically altered the entertainment as well as the learning landscape for today's young people. Television, the Internet, streaming video, Mp3s, cell phones and electronic games compete for their attention from all sides. Who knows what further novelties technology will deliver in the next decade or so? One might begin to wonder whether we will eventually need reading skills at all.

Actually, according to the Standards for the English Language Arts established by the National Council on Teachers of English (NCTE), "in order to participate fully in society and the workplace in 2020 and harness the power of technology and all its implications, we will need powerful literacy skills—at levels currently achieved by only a small percentage of the population." Our collective health, our capacity for reason, our very *future* as a connected, contributive society—and that of our fragile planet—depends upon it.

> "Readers play a more active and involved role in their communities. The decline in reading, therefore, parallels a larger retreat from participation in civic and cultural life. The long-term implication of this study not only affects literature but all the arts—as well as social activities such as volunteerism, philanthropy, and even political engagement."
>
> —Dana Gioia, Chairman, NEA, Reading at Risk

By employing the techniques outlined in the following pages with your children, you stand a good chance of helping them to discover the power and wonder inherent in books. You also stand to enrich your own relationship with them, and to help them achieve rewarding relationships with others. You may even experience a greater sense of personal fulfillment—and might just gain (or rekindle) a new appreciation for reading yourself. If nothing else, I hope these ideas ignite a new way of thinking for you and promote the discovery of your *own* ideas for unique ways to support the connection between reading and joy . . . or for that matter, between joy and *any* creative endeavor that has value and promotes pleasure and empowerment.

Ultimately, my dream is that we might reestablish a society of readers . . . and by extension, a society of thoughtful, engaged citizens who play an active, positive role in their community and their world.

Let's help our kids to access the innate joy and empowerment in exploring the ideas and insights of great writers, thinkers, artists, and philosophers. Let's imagine a world in which they actually participate, with active voices, informed opinions, and the real hope of being heard. Let's get started right now.

1

Some Whys and Hows of Reading

"You could say the age of print begat the Age of Reason which begat democracy."

—**Al Gore**, *The Assault on Reason*

A Short History of Reading

In order to fully appreciate the current and future value of reading, it is useful to take a brief look at the past.

It's been said that history began with the written word, but actually, throughout most of human history, nobody wrote—or read—at all. Although the spoken word is over six million years old, reading as we know it only emerged about six thousand years ago.

For centuries, we were an entirely oral society. Lessons were learned, records were kept, and culture was preserved via storytelling and memory. The first writings were mainly symbolic—pictures of objects and activities carved or drawn by the Sumerians in 4000 B.C. as cuneiform, and by the Egyptians as hieroglyphs. Gradually, these symbols began to develop more abstract and complex meanings, until in 2000 B.C. the Phoenicians developed the first series of symbols to represent spoken language—an alphabet made up entirely of consonants. Roughly one thousand years later, the Greeks added vowels, developing a 24-letter alphabet that is the foundation of the one we use to this day. Because the vowels were based on sounds, this alphabet made it possible to figure out words and their spelling by sounding them out. It was now possible for Greek and Roman children, along with women, slaves, and others who had been hitherto unable to do so, to learn to read and write.

Of course, the knowledge that could be gained from reading quickly translated into power, and in the medieval, religion-based society that followed, literacy became the purview of the Church and those (largely male) in positions of authority and control.

The Middle Ages in Europe saw a gradual reemergence of the written word in the wider community with the invention of lower case letters and the insertion of spaces between words. This made it possible for most readers to read silently to themselves, something which up until this point had been so unusual that those who were capable of it, such as Julius Caesar, were acknowledged in historic records on account of their ability. Most reading at this time was confined to scripture and religious texts.

"If the riches of the Indies, or the crowns of all the kingdom in Europe, were laid at my feet in exchange for my love of reading, I would spurn them all."

—Francois FéNelon

By the time of the Renaissance, the invention of printing and papermaking had brought about a commensurate rise in literacy. The age of print essentially began with the Gutenberg Bible, and reading was still undertaken primarily for religious purposes, as well as for legal, medical, and educational reasons—but legends, fables, and folktales were also popular, indicating the public's hunger for more creative, entertaining fare.

Immigrants to the North American colonies were, on average, more literate than the general population of the countries they had left, suggesting a link between literacy and a spirit of courage and curiosity. By the time of the American Revolution, the literacy rate was close to ninety percent in New England.

Between 1850 and 1950—a period that has often been cited as the high point of literacy in America—reading was not only essential to economic and class advancement, it was an important social activity. Events from the latest Dickens novel or references to Tennyson and

Shakespeare peppered social dialogue, and regular reading of fiction and poetry was taken for granted as being key to social discourse.

For the last fifty years or so, coinciding—perhaps not altogether surprisingly—with the dawn of television and later the Internet, reading has suffered a precipitous decline. Pollsters have taken an increasing interest in measuring reading habits, as well as national and global literacy rates.

There are numerous definitions of literacy. The traditional one, of course, is the ability to read and write, but the simplicity of this definition immediately begs the further question: to what degree?

Is one's name sufficient? What about road signs and basic instructions? How much must we be able to read—and write—in order to be considered literate?

The United Nations Educational, Scientific and Cultural Organization (UNESCO) puts forward the following definition: "Literacy is the ability to identify, understand, interpret, create, communicate and compute, using printed and written materials associated with varying contexts. Literacy involves a continuum of learning to enable an individual to achieve his or her goals, to develop his or her knowledge and potential, and to participate fully in the wider society."

Clearer perhaps, but still subjective. A continuum of learning to what level? Elementary school? College? Beyond? And how does one determine goals or measure human potential when these things can be so fundamentally impacted by socioeconomic status, cultural differences, or access to basic services?

An easier term to define, and possibly a clearer barometer of where we currently stand with respect to reading, is literacy's mirror image, "functional *illiteracy*"—the inability of an individual to read and write well enough to cope adequately with everyday life situations. Functionally illiterate adults cannot manage such basic tasks as filling out employment application forms, understanding a legally binding contract, or following written instructions. Moreover, functional illiteracy severely limits the ability to use a computer, mobile phone, or voting machine.

Studies conducted by the Census Bureau, the National Endowment for the Arts (NEA), the Pew Research Center, the Department of

Labor and many other bodies show that, overwhelmingly, "Americans are losing not just the will to read, but even the ability."[2]

Bottom line: Those who are functionally illiterate cannot read, write, or process and comprehend meaning beyond a fourth-grade level—that is, well enough to obtain and hold down a good job.

And this applies to over half of all Americans today.

So, what's happening?

Some Reasons for the Decline in Reading

There is a range of theories as to what is contributing most to the decline in functional literacy, and the arguments continue to rage, but the most frequent indictments are, not surprisingly, leveled at the electronic media.

Some of the strongest evidence in support of this position comes from the Netherlands, where extensive studies on leisure time were conducted between 1955 and 1995. Results showed that in the mid-'50s, when television was just being introduced, reading occupied twenty-one percent of people's spare time on weeknights and weekends, or an average of five hours a week. By the mid-'70s, TV watching had risen from an average of ten minutes a week to ten hours, while time spent reading had dropped to three and a half hours a week. By 1995, reading accounted for just nine percent of people's leisure time activities. Back in America, the NEA found a similar pattern in the results of its twenty years of research.

According to these studies, academic credentials mattered far less when it came to reading habits than whether a person had been raised in the era of television. And given the further precipitous decline in reading since the early 1990s, which saw the dawn of the Internet as well as electronic gaming and all sorts of other digital diversions, it stands to reason that these alternative entertainment choices are truly culpable. (Let's not forget, too, that the marketing budgets of these new media and technology companies vastly outweigh those of most publishing companies.) In fact, according to the A.C. Nielsen Company, the average American now watches *four hours* of television per day.

---

[2]Caleb Crain, "Twilight of the Books," *The New Yorker*.

That said, there are other factors that may have also influenced the decline in reading. The increasing pressures of meeting the bottom line force larger corporate publishing houses to spend more time focusing on sales and profit margins these days, and less on the making of art. Standards have declined, formulaic content has become the norm, and there is now a glut in the marketplace of serialized attempts to replicate the latest bestseller or popular trend. (Mercifully, there have recently been a lot of small independent companies springing up, indicating a desire among industry professionals for greater editorial freedom. Hopefully, this will soon begin to impact the sales and trends landscape, in the way that independent films have revolutionized the film industry.)

There is also fault at government level in terms of education policy, as well as within the field of education itself. Historian Harvey Graff argues that the dawn of mass schooling was actually an effort in part to *control* the degree of literacy of the working class. Ironic though it may seem, Graff suggests that the inherent dangers of a literate populace—and the potential society of radical free thinkers that might ensue—led to the advent of schooling the masses as an attempt to suppress and control literacy, rather than broaden it.

> *"Reading is more than a pastime. In today's world, it's a survival skill."*
>
> —Secretary Spellings, National Reading First Conference

Whether or not Graff's theory is true, it is clear that the No Child Left Behind Act dramatically altered the American educational landscape. With today's emphasis on standardized testing, there are days, weeks, and even months of school time being lost to meaningful, creative learning and allocated to test preparation. Teaching salaries in America continue to be shockingly low relative to the responsibilities and challenges faced by the profession, and perhaps as a result, employment standards have dropped sharply. Fourth-grade teachers in the United States now have on average five fewer years of experience than their peers in European and other countries. Budget cuts imposed upon arts-based programs in the public school system in recent years have further eroded the situation.

All the foregoing notwithstanding, my own view is that the greatest impediment to reading is a subtler, increasingly pervasive, and infinitely more powerful force.

I believe that the main reason we move away from reading as an elective activity is because of our *subconscious association*, often unwittingly learned at school and reinforced at home, between reading and "chore."

The Power of Association

I am a firm believer in the power of association. While we are physical, emotional, and spiritual beings, it is the sensory aspects of our existence that forge the connections we make in our lives. We learn *kinesthetically* (i.e., through physical experiences) from a very early age which things we connect with pleasure, and which we connect with pain. This smell reminds us of home, that sound makes us uncomfortable, this experience excites us, that one exhausts us . . . and so on.

Ideally, our early associations with reading are warm and fuzzy. We snuggle up with our parents or loved ones—in their arms, on their laps, in our beds. We nurse, suck our thumbs, guzzle a bottle, or nibble a snack while we listen to our favorite voices telling us enchanted tales, written with the intent to delight and inspire young hearts and minds. We nod off to dreamland with "visions of sugarplums dancing in our heads." It's heady stuff—who wouldn't love it? Reading = JOY.

Then we go to school.

There, we learn to read for ourselves, or at least begin to. Little by little, our parents stop reading to us, thinking their job is done, or perhaps feeling that it's better to promote our independent reading skills. Some of us struggle to develop these skills, however, and begin to associate the activity with discomfort, embarrassment, or even shame. For others, the amount of time spent reading dry, dark, or poorly written material designed to educate rather than inspire begins to create new, underlying connections between reading and boredom, frustration, and fatigue.

A subtle shift takes place in the psychic balance. *More and more, the act of reading becomes associated with pressure, deadlines and responsibility—and less and less with* joy.

Our challenge is to reverse that trend.

The Strategies

2

Babies and Toddlers: Sowing the Seeds for a Love of Reading

"Reading aloud to young children is so critical that the American Academy of Pediatrics recommends that doctors prescribe reading activities along with other advice given to parents at regular checkups."

—**American Academy of Pediatrics**

When should we *start* reading to our children?

Short answer—as soon as we start talking to them.

Doctors and nurses trained through the pediatric literacy nonprofit Reach Out and Read (www.reachoutandread.org) have actually been "prescribing" books since 1989. Reach Out and Read's Medical Director, Perri Klass, MD, says, "Reading aloud to children helps their brains develop, and it gives parents and children a wonderful loving way to spend time together." And Reading Is Fundamental, the oldest and largest family literacy organization in America (www.rif.org), states that: "children develop much of their capacity for learning in the first three years of life, when their brains grow to 90% of their eventual adult weight. When parents talk, sing, and read to their child, links among the child's brain cells are strengthened and new cells and links are formed. Many pediatricians believe that a child who has never held a book or listened to a story is not a fully healthy child."

Indeed, there's quite a bit of evidence to support the idea of starting to read to a baby in utero. Studies done at the University of North Carolina, in which pregnant women recited specific paragraphs of a children's story three times a day for the last two and half months of their pregnancy, showed a marked preference among newborns (improved sucking rate when nursing, increased heart rate) for the familiar passages, even when read by an unfamiliar voice. These experiments established that a fetus is able to become familiar with certain sounds while in utero, and to begin to associate those tones with a sense of comfort and security.

Babies love to hear the rhythms and intonations of a beloved adult's voice. Poetry and rhyming text can be especially attractive to the infant ear, and babies are also naturally drawn in by bright, eye-catching artwork. Getting them used to the idea of looking at and listening to books as early as possible, *especially when supported by an activity that connects reading with pleasure,* such as cuddling or nursing, is a significant first step in helping a child become an enthusiastic reader in later life.

Creating the Connections

The following ideas focus on establishing an early association between reading and joy, and most of them are equally applicable across all age groups. By harnessing the power of suggestion and subliminal association, these actions will send subtle, non-verbal messages to your child about the value and pleasure of reading, thereby providing the foundation for an appetite for reading in later life. Let's begin with two overarching ideas that form the foundation on which everything else is based:

> *"Read-aloud has the power not only to sustain but also to resuscitate an interest in and affection for the printed word for children of all ages."*
>
> —Esmé Raji Codell,
> *How to Get Your Child to Love Reading*

1. Start reading to your child as early— and as often—as possible. It doesn't have to take a lot of time. Look for opportunities to read together in the course of your daily routine: first thing on waking, during mealtime, at nap times or bedtime, while in the bath, etc. Spend plenty of time talking and singing to babies as well! Bear in mind that it's vitally important that Dads read with children as well as Moms. The vast majority of pre-school teachers are female, and young children—especially boys—need the positive male role modeling with respect to reading that Dads can provide. Of course, grandparents, siblings, and other loved ones make great readers too—and should also be encouraged to do so as often as possible.

2. Set a good example! Granted, the pressures of daily life—not to mention parenting—can sorely limit our ability to carve out time for ourselves, but try to let your children see you engaged in reading whenever possible . . . ideally books, but newspapers and article-based magazines are fine too. Nothing will teach children to love reading more than seeing the adults around them showing enthusiasm for it. In fact, according to a recent survey by Scholastic, parents who regularly read for pleasure are *six* times more likely to have kids who read for fun. Give your children the visual cue and the underlying emotional message that reading is an important and enjoyable activity that the significant adults in their lives value.

Having established these two keys, the following ideas are divided into three sections: things you can do **In the Home**, when it's just you and your child; activities to link a love of reading to people, places, and events **Beyond the Home**; and suggestions as to **What to Read**. Some of these ideas may overlap, or sit equally comfortably under another heading, and hopefully they will stimulate further ideas that you can introduce, depending on your particular circumstances and the opportunities that you are presented with.

In the Home

Provide a warm and inviting "reading atmosphere." While you'll probably be waiting forever for the perfect moment—and it's more important to read in less-than-ideal conditions than not at all—distractions such as loud background noises, harsh lighting, or myriad other factors can serve to undermine your best efforts. Look for opportunities to read with your child at times and in places that associate reading with all things "warm and fuzzy."

Nurse or cuddle while you read. This is one of the most powerful kinesthetic ways to help children develop a subconscious association between reading and feelings of warmth, joy, and love. The synapses and connections that are formed here make up the foundation for joyful reading later in life.

Offer your child something to hold, play with, or chew on while reading. Teething discomfort can disrupt even the most attentive listener. Noshing on a teething ring, biscuit, or other baby-safe snack, or playing with a favorite toy, can often help babies to listen and enjoy the experience more fully. Active toddlers may find it easier to listen to stories if their hands are occupied. If your toddler won't sit still for reading time, try offering crayons and paper or a snack to engage them while you read.

Build "reading time" into your daily routine. Set aside at least one regularly scheduled time each day for reading together. Babies thrive on routine, and this will quickly become important "together" time that both you and your child will look forward to.

Create a "reading ritual." Human beings are creatures of habit. Throughout our lives, we build a store of conditioned responses to experiences—we smell a lemon, our mouth waters. We hear a fire alarm, our heart rate increases and we jump into action. This device (also called "Pavlovian response" or "conditioned reflex") can be, and often is, used in our favor, for example by pro athletes, trainers, and high-powered performers and executives who work to build a desired conditioned response to a prompt. Establishing some kind of physical ritual, whether it's a sight (the turning on of a warm, friendly reading lamp, for instance) or a sound (anything from a gentle chime to the words "story time!") just before settling in for a good story can be a powerful tool in cultivating eager anticipation for the pleasure of reading, both now and in your child's later life.

> *"The more that you read,*
> *the more things you will know.*
> *The more that you learn,*
> *the more places you'll go."*
>
> —Dr. Seuss

Return to favorites as often as possible. Notice which books your baby really seems to be responding to, and return to them frequently. As he or she becomes more familiar with the text and pictures, you can then deepen the experience by pointing out details, asking questions, etc. This is an important way to send your child the subliminal message that you value and honor their preferences and interests. In the words of the wonderful French author and teacher Daniel Pennac, "To re-read is not necessarily to repeat. To re-read is to provide fresh proof of enduring love."

Provide magnetic letters for the fridge, vinyl or foam tub letters for the bath, and alphabet puzzles, blocks, and games. Surround your child with the alphabet. Let him or her explore the textures, shapes and sounds of the letters (with your support) in the spirit of play and adventure, and watch how easily reading unfolds.

Keep books *everywhere*. Make sure books are readily available for any opportunity that may arise: In addition to the bookshelves in our kids' rooms and playroom, we keep baskets or stacks of books in the bathroom, living room, kitchen—even in a tote in the car. This makes a powerful visual and emotional statement for a child about the value of reading in family life.

Visit libraries and bookstores as often as possible. Good libraries and bookstores can be delicious sensory experiences, rich with the unique smells, texture,s and visual delights that books provide. Most of them have children's sections, with child-size tables and chairs or cushions and other support materials, and as such, they are wonderful places for children to explore and experience the magic of books. Many offer a regular story hour, book-based activities, and visiting authors or artists programs. Get your child his or her own library card as soon as the library's policy allows, or frequent buyer card at your local bookstore. Put your family's name on their mailing lists for special events, and enjoy the many opportunities these important facilities can provide.

Encourage books as gifts. Invite grandparents and other family members and friends to give books to your children as gifts. In this way, the value of books is underscored, and your child begins to develop his or her own library.

Look for reading opportunities on outings. When out and about with your baby or toddler, bring books along to read while waiting for an appointment, at the playground, or just for your child to look at while in the stroller. Also, be aware of opportunities to point out signs, posters, and other reading-related materials and explore them together.

What to Read

The following are age-appropriate reading recommendations for babies and toddlers:

Soft books, bath books, and board books. When our son, Sam, was an infant, my husband and I found some extra-large, cuddly "books" with only two or three pages of soft, colorful artwork and no text. The pictures were quilted and textured, adding dimension and interest, and when Sam was in his stroller or baby seat, or while we were making dinner perhaps, we would often prop the soft book open in front of him. He would stare and coo at the pages, and we would periodically turn them for him when it seemed he was losing interest. I'll never forget the thrill of seeing him reach out and turn the page for himself the first time. We also had soft waterproof books for the bath, which we read with both our children while we bathed them and which they loved to hold and chew on.

Board books are also terrific tactile experiences for babies and toddlers. Their sturdiness and small size make it easy for very young children to handle them, turning the pages so they feel like they are "reading" for themselves. These types of early books offer important visual and tactile reinforcement of the idea that books are both valuable and fun.

Books about babies and toddlers, animals, and familiar objects and activities. Babies and toddlers particularly enjoy pictures—whether photographic or illustrated—of their world in all its glorious detail. Help them begin to grasp the concept of connecting words to images by pointing to and naming the items featured: *"Where's the baby?"* *"See the spoon?"* etc. Books about familiar activities, such as bathing, eating, or sleeping are especially effective.

Books with only a few words or one or two lines of text per page, and bright, colorful eye-catching illustrations. Choose those that feature pictures and names of objects familiar to your child, and books with simple storylines that are easy for the youngest listener to follow.

Books about animals, especially familiar ones, like farm animals. Again, help your child begin to grasp the concept of connecting words to images by pointing to and naming the items featured: *"There's a cow! What does the cow say?"*

Rhyming or poetry books. Books that provide fun sounds and rhythms quickly engage the infant ear. Ideally, choose those that have equally engaging artwork. The great reading specialist Jim Trelease, in his *The Read-Aloud Handbook*, suggests that rhyme "echoes the first sound a child falls in love with—the rhythmic, rhyming beat-beat-beat of a mother's heart." Trelease adds, "Children find pleasure in words that rhyme for the same reason humans subconsciously enjoy looking at stripes and plaids or listening to musical harmony—they help to arrange a chaotic world."

Books that invite physical exploration. Textures to touch, flaps to lift, tabs to pull, holes to peek through or poke fingers in and are all terrific tools to introduce the concept of books as being truly "interactive."

Homemade books and photo albums with pictures of family members and friends. Babies and toddlers *love* to look at photographs, especially of people, places and things they know. Pick up a small photo album (4" × 6" or 5" × 7" is ideal) and fill it with photos of family members (including your child), friends, your home, pets, and familiar objects. Try to choose pictures that feature no more than one or two people or items at a time, so that the images are large, clear, and specific. If you have the digital know-how, you can scan the photos into a document along with captions under each picture in order to begin the association for your child between pictures and words. You can then print the pages and bind them with ribbon or paste them into an album or notebook. You'll be amazed at the level of interest your child will show, and at the joy a simple, personalized book like this can bring them.

> "The world of books is the most remarkable creation of man: nothing else that he builds ever lasts. Monuments fall; nations perish; civilizations grow old and die out; new races build others. But in the world of books are volumes that have seen this happen again and again and yet live on. Still young, still as fresh as the day they were written, still telling men's hearts, of the hearts of men centuries dead."
>
> —Clarence Day

ABC and counting books, for beginning associations with numbers and letters. Choose those with vibrant, colorful artwork or accompanying storytelling or rhyming text.

Think beyond books! The National Assessment of Educational Progress (NAEP) also found a positive relationship between students' average reading scores and how many different *types* of reading materials they had at home—including newspapers, magazines, and encyclopedias.

A magazine can make for fun reading with a baby or toddler. Choose those that have a lot of pictures and relate to an apparent or potential area of interest—animals, trucks, other children, etc. See what ideas for stories you can find inside, or even make up from the pictures. The important thing is to spend time sitting with children, turning pages and discovering the joy of reading in all its forms, together.

There is, in fact, a magazine geared especially towards babies and toddlers. *Babybug*, made by the publishers of *Cricket* magazine (Carus Publishing), is "the listening and looking magazine for infants and toddlers, just right for small hands. It's filled with simple stories and rhymes and bright, engaging pictures that babies and parents will delight in sharing again and again."

Reading Techniques

You don't have to be a born performer to engage your young audience in a story . . . but there are a few simple tricks of the trade that can go a long way toward inviting better listening skills and improving the experience for both of you. As with Creating the Connection, there are two overarching ideas to keep in mind at all times:

1. **Invite participation.** Encourage your young listener to join in. Toddlers love to participate—ask them to turn pages, make sounds, repeat words or phrases, lift flaps, name things, and point to pictures or details. It's all about interactivity.

2. **Enlist other family members and loved ones—*especially* Dads and older siblings—to be "readers."** If you're fortunate enough to be in this position, having big brothers and sisters read to littler ones is a terrific way to provide the youngest with a role model and the oldest with a chance to improve their skills and shine. But any beloved family member, caregiver, or friend who takes the time to share a story with your child will further reinforce the value and pleasure of reading. And as I said before, it's especially important for fathers to read to and with their children as much as possible, to provide as much positive male role modeling when it comes to reading as you can.

In addition...

Read with "color" in your voice. While you needn't put on a performance, keeping your voice alive and interesting can make all the difference in terms of a young child's ability to concentrate and follow a story.

Experiment with emphasis here, enthusiasm there, tenderness in another place. Find the cadence or rhythm of the author's language, and try to convey the mood or the characters' intentions. Don't yuck it up so much that the listener pays more attention to your vocal acrobatics than the words or the story, but do try to avoid a monotone delivery. Keep it alive!

Point to, describe, and ask about things in the pictures. Draw your baby's attention to details, familiar objects, colors, etc. Ask *"Where's the . . .?"* or *"Can you show me the . . .?"* This encourages him or her to begin to experience books as an interactive, as opposed to a passive, experience and lays the groundwork for imaginative and emotional participation when reading.

> *"Outside of a dog, a book is man's best friend. Inside of a dog, it's too dark to read."*
>
> —Groucho Marx

Gauge your baby's interest level as you go, and either move the story along a little, linger on a page, or stop as needed. It's no crime to skip over or condense a few sentences while reading to a very young child. The most important thing is to maintain their interest. Take your cue from them, and adjust accordingly. If your baby starts to get wriggly, it's probably time to put the book away and find another activity— quit while you're ahead. If they seem fascinated by something on a particular page, linger there and engage in dialogue about it. If there's a picture or some element that seems to trouble them, skip over it.

When our daughter, Hope, was tiny, she was fascinated by a book called *Daddy's Lullaby* (Tony Bradman/Jason Cockcroft). She clearly loved the story and the beautiful watercolor illustrations of the baby and her family—but when we got to the page where the Daddy sings, *"Hush little baby, don't you cry..."* Hope's lower lip would quiver and she'd burst into tears. She wanted to keep reading the book— she kept reaching for it and choosing it, again and again—just not *that* page. Something about the song—whether it was the lyric or the minor key, we still don't know—saddened her greatly. So we skipped over that part for a while and began to include it again when she seemed ready for it.

Emma's Family Favorites for Babies and Toddlers

"Voracious readers are made, not born. No child is born loving baseball or pizza; they learn to like what they see their parents liking."

—**Bernice E. Cullinan,**
Read to Me: Raising Kids Who Love to Read

Many parents don't read—or even talk much—to their infants, because they think they are too young to understand. This is backwards thinking. In fact, talking, singing, and reading to your baby are *how* he or she learns language.

There are many wonderful resources for parents to learn more about the critical role we play in our child's brain development: Zero to Three's website (www.zerotothree.org) is a great place to start, as are the books and websites of T. Berry Brazelton (www.touchpoints.org) and Drs. William and Jim Sears (www.askdrsears.com). Other personal favorites of mine include books by Penelope Leach, The Gesell Institute's Child Development Series, *Mothering* magazine, and Rob Reiner's *I Am Your Child* DVD's, available through www.parentsaction-store.org.

The following is a list of books for infants, babies, and toddlers that continue to be time-tested favorites:

***Biscuit* series** (Alyssa Satin Capucilli)
The adventures of a lovable pup and the little girl who owns him. Picture books, Lift-the-Flaps, and I Can Reads.

Blue Hat, Green Hat (Sandra Boynton)
Anything by Sandra Boynton is a laugh a minute—but this one, featuring a chicken with a mixed-up clothes sense, is a special favorite.

Brown Bear, Brown Bear, What Do You See? (Bill Martin Jr./Eric Carle)
A wonderful introduction to animals and colors, told in rhyme, with the incomparable artwork of Eric Carle.

Chicka Chicka Boom Boom (Bill Martin Jr./John Archambault/Lois Ehlert)
Infectious rhythm and rhyme, vibrant art. Great for teaching the alphabet, including uppercase and lowercase letters.

Counting Kisses (Karen Katz)
Count-and-kiss along as each family member kisses baby goodnight.

Caterpillar's Wish (Mary Murphy)
Caterpillar wishes she could fly with her best friends, bee and lady-bug—and one day she just may! Vibrant colors, simple text, and a sweet, affirming story.

Daddy's Lullaby (Tony Bradman/Jason Cockcroft)
Arriving home late from work, Daddy finds everyone in the family sleeping soundly . . . except baby. Together they walk, rock, and sing until they fall asleep.

Dr. Seuss's ABC (Dr. Seuss)
The best—and silliest—ABC of all. Sure to bring about smiles and learning with every repeat reading.

> **One Fish, Two Fish, Red Fish, Blue Fish**—*". . . from there to here, from here to there, funny things are everywhere!" Dr. Seuss at his early-childhood best.*

> **Mr. Brown Can Moo! Can You?**—*There isn't a sound Mr. Brown can't do, from a hippo's gum chewing to a goldfish's kiss. Giggles—and sound effects—galore.*

> **The Foot Book**—*Dr. Seuss's "Wacky Book of Opposites."*

Go, Dog. Go! (P.D. Eastman)
A Seuss-style classic that teaches colors, shapes, language, and diversity in one simple, funny tale.

Goodnight, Moon (Margaret Wise Brown/Clement Hurd)
A little rabbit preparing for bed says goodnight to everyone and everything in his world. The perfect, classic bedtime story.

> **The Runaway Bunny**—*A little bunny's imaginary hide-and-seek game with his Mom, who finds him, reassuringly, each time.*

Guess How Much I Love You (Sam McBratney/Anita Jeram)
A heartwarming tale, featuring the beloved Little Nutbrown Hare and Big Nutbrown Hare, and celebrating familial love with humor and insight.

Happy Birth Day! (Robie Harris/Michael Emberley)
A Mom tells of baby's first 24 hours of life outside the womb, and shows how loved children are from the very start.

Maisy series (Lucy Cousins)
Simple stories about an endearing mouse and her friends, told in large print with colorful illustrations.

Max and Ruby series (Rosemary Wells)
Rosemary Wells' classic bunny duo (and hit TV series): Ever-patient big sister Ruby and her impossible, irrepressible baby brother, Max.

Mr. Men and Little Miss series (Roger Hargreaves)
Child-size paperbacks featuring such lovable characters as Mr. Happy, Mr. Messy, Mr. Shy, Little Miss Trouble, and Little Miss Perfect—with simple, brightly colored line drawings children love.

My Very First Mother Goose (Iona Opie (Editor)/
Rosemary Wells)
Those familiar and beloved staples of childhood verse, bursting with new life.

The Naughty Ducklings (Stewart Crowly/Susi Adams)
A group of ducklings explore the world in this charming "magic-window board book" that reveals new images through each windowed page.

Pat the Bunny (Dorothy Kunhardt)
One of the very first "interactive" books, originally published in 1940—but as beloved today by babies everywhere as they play peek-a-boo, try on Mommy's ring, and, of course, pat the bunny.

Read-Aloud Rhymes for the Very Young (Jack Prelutsky/Marc Brown)
Two hundred poems selected by one America's best-loved poets, with a foreword on reading aloud by Jim Trelease and art by Marc Brown of "Arthur"—what could be better?

Sam's Little Sister (Yves Got)
Sam loves his little sister, even when she doesn't get everything right. Kids do, too, and are reassured by the gentle lessons on sibling rivalry—and devotion—that Sam and his sister provide.

The Very Hungry Caterpillar (Eric Carle)
A caterpillar munches his way to butterfly-hood in this beloved classic from the masterful Eric Carle.

The Wheels on the Bus (Paul O. Zelinsky)
The wheels on the bus actually do go round and round, and the windows go up and down, and everything works in this wonderful, interactive adaptation of the classic song—complete with sub-plots hidden within the illustrations.

Where's Spot?—(The *Spot* series) (Eric Hill)
Babies can lift the flaps, chew on board books, and learn to read with the simple tales of Spot the puppy and his friends and family.

You Can Name One 100 Trucks! (Jim Becker, Andy Mayer/Randy Chewning)
One of Sam's early and enduring favorites—and indeed, he could name all 100 of them.

and *any* books by . . .

>   Sandra Boynton
>   Eric Carle
>   Dr. Seuss
>   Rosemary Wells
>   Margaret Wise Brown

3

Preschoolers: Cultivating the Joy of Reading

"If every parent understood the huge educational benefits and intense happiness brought about by reading aloud to children, and if every parent—and every adult caring for a child—read aloud a minimum of three stories a day to the children in their lives, we could probably wipe out illiteracy within one generation."

—Mem Fox, bestselling children's book author and literacy expert

The single most important thing we can do to help our children grow into thoughtful, compassionate, *literate* adults is to read aloud to them.

Reading aloud initiates a vital, ongoing process of brain development in young people, and lays the groundwork that enables them to enjoy reading for themselves as they get older.

In fact, children who are read to at least three times a week by a family member are almost *twice* as likely to score in the top twenty-five percent in reading as children who are read to less, according to the Early Childhood Longitudinal Study, sponsored by the U.S. Department of Education, National Center for Education Statistics, and other federal organizations.

Despite this and other well-documented facts, only *fifty percent* of parents are reported to actually read to their children.

Justifications abound: "I don't have time," "I'm not a good reader myself," "My child doesn't seem that interested." Truth is, though, there are few more important gifts we can give our children than helping them to discover the joy, freedom, and power of reading. And it needn't be a hugely time-consuming or daunting task...actually, just a few minutes each day, *especially* when supported by an effort to connect reading with *pleasure*, is all it takes to sow the seeds of an enthusiastic reader.

Building the Connections

The following ideas focus on reinforcing the connection between reading and pleasure through the power of suggestion and subliminal association. The subtle messages these actions send about the value of reading are the foundation of the more active, creative endeavors to follow.

As with babies and toddlers, the most important things we can do to continue to build the connection between reading and pleasure for preschoolers are:

1. Continue reading to—and with—your child. Reading together through the preschool years is critical. It helps children become better readers themselves, aids them in discovering which kinds of stories and authors inspire them, and provides important opportunities for them to explore social and moral issues together with their loved ones.

2. Continue to set a good example by letting your child see the significant adults in his or her life reading whenever possible.

In the Home

As detailed in the previous chapter, continue to:

- ✍ **Provide a warm and inviting "reading atmosphere,"** free of visual or aural distractions.

- ✍ **Build reading time into your daily routine.** It doesn't matter if it's at bedtime, bath-time, or whenever—as long as it's consistent.

- ✍ **Maintain a "reading ritual,"** such as a sound or sight cue to promote anticipation.

- ✍ **Return to favorites as often as possible.** Young children *need* repeated readings in order to really grasp a book's language and meaning.

- ✍ **Provide letters for the fridge or tub, and alphabet toys, games, and puzzles,** along with other environmental aids that promote reading, such as posters or book-related artwork in bedrooms and playrooms.

- ✍ **Keep books *everywhere*.** In the bathroom, living room, kitchen—even in the car. Make a visual and emotional statement about the value of reading in family life.

- ✍ **Cuddle while you read.** The most powerful kinesthetic way to help children subconsciously associate reading with joy and love is to snuggle up and share the pleasure together.

In addition…

Be sensitive to timing with respect to choice of material. It's a good idea to select books at bedtime that you know won't leave unsettling images or thoughts in your child's mind prior to turning off the light. Save those books for earlier in the day, when there is plenty of time to discuss and/or process the reactions and questions that may arise.

> *"Without books, God is silent, justice dormant, natural science at a stand, philosophy lame, letters dumb, and all things involved in darkness."*
>
> —Thomas Bartholin

Create a "Book Nook" or "Reading Corner." When Sam was small, we put a big, comfy beanbag chair in a corner of his room near the bookshelf, with a floor lamp next to it and an assortment of stuffed animals inviting him to snuggle in and read with them. Often we read to him there, but it was always a thrill to catch him snuggled up there on his own, leafing through the pages of a favorite book.

Organize books attractively on shelves or in baskets. This demonstrates respect for them, and makes it much easier to find the one you or child may be looking for at any given moment. Try arranging them according to size, author, title, genre, subject—whatever makes it easiest for you and your child to manage, and to find beloved favorites quickly. Cluttered piles send a negative message—and can undermine your best efforts if you are unable to put your hand on a requested book within a reasonable amount of time.

Experiment with displays. Try displaying books the way classrooms, libraries and bookstores do—with the books' covers facing out, as opposed to the spine. This simple adjustment can make a big difference in whether your child is drawn to selecting books to look at or read on his or her own initiative. Rotate them regularly for maximum interest—and experiment with arranging displays according to season, topic, genre, or theme.

Enroll your child in a Book-of-the-Month club. There are many variations on book clubs, but the premise is pretty much the same: Once a month, your child will receive a special book selection in the mail, appropriate for his or her age group and at a discounted price. My kids still get excited when that familiar package arrives—another way to underscore the association between books and pleasure!

> *"Good children's literature appeals not only to the child in the adult, but to the adult in the child."*
>
> —Anonymous

Parents have the opportunity to review each month's selection before it is sent, so they may opt out, elect not to receive a book one month, or change the current selection at any time. Most clubs also offer a points-based reward system, so that for every so many books bought, you are entitled to complimentary or dramatically discounted "bonus" books.

One club worth exploring is **Children's Book of the Month Club** (www.cbomc.com). Scholastic also offers a number of kids' book club options (www.scholastic.com).

Surprise your child occasionally with an impromptu present. Finding a new book under the pillow or on the breakfast table—whether from a bookstore, library, yard sale, or book swap with a friend—can be an inexpensive way to surprise and delight your child. It lets them know you were thinking of them, and connects books with the joy of receiving a gift.

***Never* withhold books or use them as a threat.** Although it may seem like a natural consequence, saying something like "If you don't behave, no bedtime story tonight!" turns books into weapons and quickly creates negative associations where you are trying to build positive ones.

Beyond the Home

Continue to employ the suggestions from the previous chapter, including:

- **Visit libraries and bookstores as often as possible.** Expose your child as often as possible to the delicious sensory experiences—the smells, textures, and visual delights—that books provide. Inquire about story hours, book-based activities, and visiting authors or artists programs. Get your child his or her own library card as soon as the library's policy allows, or frequent buyer card at your local bookstore, and put your family's name on mailing lists for special events. (Remember, public libraries are *free!*)

- **Encourage the giving of books as gifts** by grandparents and other family members and friends, ensuring that your child will never be short of a good read.

- **Look for reading opportunities on outings,** while waiting for appointments, at the playground, etc. Also, look for opportunities to point out signs, posters, and other reading-related materials.

In addition…

Involve your child in performing and visual arts programs. Studies show that students who actively participate in the arts—whether studying a particular discipline, such as music or acting, or attending the theater, museums, concerts, and other arts-based events and activities on a regular basis—are *twice* as likely to read for pleasure as those who do not. They are also three times more likely to win awards for academic achievement at school.

Actions and Activities

The following activities are designed not only to reinforce the joy but also to underscore the potential empowerment of reading. They have been divided into four areas: **Supporting Your Child;**

Encouraging Exploration; Skill Building; and **Beyond the Home**. Try as many as you like, and let them serve as a springboard for your own creative ideas and activities.

The overarching aim of all these actions and activities is to:

Connect reading with life skills. Routinely show your children how reading skills affect our lives by inviting them to participate in life and household management in as many ways as possible. For instance, you might:

- Read a recipe out aloud while you cook together.
- Read and interpret the directions or manual together as you assemble equipment or games, or make household repairs.
- Read shopping lists and package ingredients together while grocery shopping.
- Take your children with you when you vote!

These actions make your kids feel like important and contributive members of the family, while building reading skills at the same time.

Supporting Your Child

Offer books as problem solvers. A well-written and well-timed book that addresses an issue your child is wrestling with can be a godsend to you both. "Bibliotherapy" offers reassurance to your child that he or she is not alone, and can also provide new ideas for coping strategies as well as some comic relief. It also teaches your child to turn to books for answers to questions or problems in later life. Some examples:

- Blankie issues? Read *Owen* (Kevin Henkes) or *D.W.'s Lost Blankie* (Marc Brown).
- Tattling? Try *Armadillo Tattletale* (Helen Ketteman).
- Mealtime struggles? *Bread and Jam for Frances* (Russell and Lillian Hoban) might just do the trick.
- Potty training? Look at *Once Upon a Potty* (Alona Frankel) or *Oh No, Gotta Go!* (Susan Middleton Elya/G. Brian Karas).
- Trip to the hospital? Check out Ludwig Bemelmans' classic, *Madeline*.

- Bullying or Teasing? Read *Stand Tall, Molly Lou Melon* (Patty Lovell, David Catrow) or *Chrysanthemum* (Kevin Henkes).

A wonderful resource for more ideas in this regard is *Books to Grow With: A Guide to Using the Best Children's Fiction for Everyday Issues and Tough Challenges* by Cheryl Coon.

You can also ask your local librarian or bookseller for recommendations... or log on to an Internet bookseller such as www.amazon.com and enter the topic or issue at hand in the search bar.

Experiment with support activities. This is one of my favorite ways to enrich a literary experience: Look for activities that build on and support the ideas or themes within your child's favorite books. Bake a recipe, build a model, or play a game inspired by a story. Visit a place mentioned, or attend a relevant museum exhibit. Listen to music, watch a TV program, or see a movie that expands on a theme or topic.

For example, does your child enjoy *The Little Engine That Could* (Watty Piper/Loren Long)?

Why not:

- Build a model train together.
- Screen the animated version of *The Little Engine That Could* or Walt Disney's *Dumbo*, in which the circus train says *"I think I can, I think I can..."* while climbing a mountain.
- Laugh over Shel Silverstein's parody "The Little Engine That Couldn't" (a.k.a. "The Little Blue Engine") which gives the story a decidedly more pessimistic ending.
- Listen to train songs—www.railserve.com provides a list of recommended CDs and recordings of songs about trains and railroads by various well-known artists.
- Pay a visit to a railroad museum.
- Visit the **"I Think I Can Railroad Tour."** A full-size replica of The Little Engine That Could makes an annual circuit around the United States. Arranged through Rail Events, Inc., a number of museum and railroad operations host the "I Think I Can Tour"—for more information, visit www.thelittleenginethatcouldtour.com.

- Explore railroad art—classic paintings, photographs, and posters of steam trains, locomotives, and the like at galleries, museums, and libraries, and in books or online.

- Pick up a wooden train whistle from a toy store, along with a conductor's cap, and make a family "train" with your child, chugging around the house or garden.

- Take advantage of the book's references to encourage your child to eat spinach and drink milk as "good things for girls and boys!"

The possibilities are limited only by your imagination.

For more ideas, check out:

- *Crafts from Your Favorite Fairy Tales* (Kathy Ross)

- *Story S-t-r-e-t-c-h-e-r-s: Activities to Expand Children's Favorite Books* (Shirley C. Raines and Robert J. Canady)

- www.thebestkidsbooksite.com—"An Interactive Media Channel where Books, Crafts, Podcasts, Online Video, and Web Resources Intersect"

- http://family.go.com/entertainment/pkg-crafts/—for craft ideas

Or simply start by conducting an Internet search (using Google or any other search engine provider) on a beloved book or story title, and see where it takes you. Ask your librarian for even more resources.

Advocate for and/or support reading and literacy activities at school. Book fairs and author visits can begin as early as preschool, and most preschool programs welcome visiting readers. Ask if you can come in and read a story to the class, and consider incorporating a related activity the children can do together after the story is over.

Encouraging Exploration

Make up your own stories. You don't have to be a writer to make up stories from scratch—young children are very forgiving of plot inconsistencies! Travel time, bath time, and waiting time are all great opportunities for storytelling, even without a book in hand. Turn something your child did recently into a story that he or she stars in. Retell fairytales or classic stories, perhaps relocating or contemporizing them, or substituting names or other characters (think "Fractured Fairy Tales").

Encourage your child to draw pictures of a story. Even if a book is already illustrated, you can invite children to draw their own ideas about a story—a personal take on the characters, for instance, or pictures that convey feelings the book generates for them. For children who are very visual, putting their reactions to what they hear on paper can be a wonderful way to internalize the story.

Record your voice reading a favorite story. Make your own audiobook for your child that he or she can play when you're not around, perhaps following along in the book itself. Simply record yourself reading the story aloud on a cassette or CD (strictly for your own home use, of course—anything else is a copyright infringement). This can be especially helpful as a transition to sleep at bedtime, and is also a great way to stay connected with—and reading to—your child if you have to be away for any length of time.

Play storytelling games. Start a story with one or two sentences yourself, then encourage your child to make up the next, followed by more from you, and so on. You might also write down stories your child tells you, reinforcing the connection between word and print.

Try a "storytime" play date or party theme. Invite two or three of your child's friends over for a storytelling session. You might make it a daytime pajama party, asking the kids to come in PJs or nighties, and to bring a favorite story or stuffed animal. Provide milk and cookies, blankets, and pillows and snuggle in for a delicious hour of read-aloud. Or you might center a play date on a specific story or series of stories, which you then expand upon with story-related activities, crafts, snacks, etc.

Write to your children! Even if they can't read yet, this is a simple way to encourage and incorporate more reading into your children's lives, and to underscore its value as a communications tool. Lunch notes are a great way to begin this tradition, and to connect reading with love. With the help of a willing preschool teacher, a simple *"Thinking of you! Hope you're having a great day! XO"* can be a great joy for a child to "read." Once a child is reading independently, write notes to convey information (*"There is chocolate milk in this fridge!"*), to provide friendly reminders of events or tasks (*"Wet towels need to be* *hung up, please!"*) or just as a means of expressing affection, and stick them in backpacks, under pillows, on the fridge or mirror, etc.

Skill Building

Tell stories about when *you* were a child. Children love to know what their parents did when they were little, and this is a wonderful way to reinforce the concept and delight of storytelling. It also encourages them to view their *own* "life story" with new perspective.

Help your kids make their own books. Even the youngest children can experience the thrill of writing their own story or making their own book. Take a few blank sheets of paper, cut them into quarters, then punch holes along the longer side and tie the "book" together with ribbon or string. Invite your child to write a title and draw a picture on the front. Then, on each left page they can write a word, sentence, or more, while on the right page they can draw and color an illustration, or perhaps cut and paste a picture from a magazine.

> *"From your parents you learn love and laughter and how to put one foot before the other. But when books are opened you discover that you have wings."*
>
> —Helen Hayes, actress

For younger children, ask them to tell you a story that you write down for them. Then you can illustrate it together, either with drawings or by cutting out pictures from magazines. You can also buy blank spiral or bound sketchbooks for your child to write stories in.

There are several companies (Creations by You, makers of the Oppenheim Award-winning *"Illustory Make Your Own Story Kit,"* www.cafepress.com, www.thinkitinkitpublishing.com, and www.shutterfly.com are a few examples) that will actually print and bind books for you that look very professional. You can even take it a step further and self-publish your child's work with a print-on-demand company, such as www.lulu.com or www.iuniverse.com.

Play word games together. Games like Scrabble® and Boggle® are obviously terrific ways to strengthen reading (and spelling) skills, and both make "junior" versions for preschoolers. There are many other wonderful games that provide the same degree of learning while strengthening the correlation between reading and fun. From Monopoly® to Clue® to Trivial Pursuit®, board games of all kinds are important and valuable alternatives to television and electronic games. "Homegrown" games like "I Spy" are also good ways to strengthen literacy skills while providing essential family together time. Try one night a week TV-free, and play games instead.

Cook with your child. Creating and enjoying foods inspired by stories is a wonderful way to build on the association between reading and pleasure, and to bring books to life. You can make a concoction you find in a favorite book—"Three Bears" porridge (a.k.a. oatmeal), "If You Give A Mouse a Cookie" chocolate chip cookies (or "Pig Pancakes" or "Moose Muffins"), "Green Eggs and Ham," etc. There are a number of literature-related cookbooks that can further integrate cooking with reading—check out:

- *The Mother Goose Cookbook* (Marianna Mayer)
- *Storybook Stew* (Suzanne Barchers & Peter Rauen)
- *Once Upon a Recipe* (Karen Green)
- *Book Cooks* (Cheryl Apgar)
- *Fanny at Chez Panisse: A Child's Restaurant Adventures with 46 Recipes* (Alice L. Waters) and
- *Recipes for Reading* (Gwynne Spencer), among others.

Of course, simply reading recipes and labels together while you create something delicious is a subliminal way to reinforce reading (and math!) skills, and to strengthen the connection between reading and pleasure. Try creating a family cookbook together, filled with favorite recipes that your child can illustrate.

Beyond the Home

See a movie (or play) based on a book. Many classic children's books have been translated to film or stage—some more successfully than others, of course. Whether you read the book or see the film or play first, you can explore the differences in the story as it gets translated from page to stage or screen, as well as the ways in which the characters or scenes did or did not match your child's imagined version of the story.

Some of our family favorites when my kids were in preschool were:

- *Alice in Wonderland* (from the original book by Lewis Carroll)
- *Cinderella* (from Brothers Grimm)

- *The Little Mermaid* (from Hans Christian Andersen)
- *The 101 Dalmatians* (from Dodie Smith)
- *Peter Pan* (from J.M. Barrie)
- *Shrek* (from William Steig)
- *The Wizard of Oz* (from L. Frank Baum)

Listen to books on tape or CD, or download them to your MP3 player. A growing body of research is showing that listening is just as effective as reading with the eyes, and supports the use of audiobooks to enhance fluency and comprehension. The many benefits of audiobooks include:

- Augmenting teachers' and parents' ability to read with their children
- Introducing new vocabulary
- Providing demonstrations of fluent reading as well as phrasing and articulation
- Offering access to books a reader may be unable to read independently
- Creating greater opportunities for discussion and comprehension
- Supporting struggling readers by helping them relax into the story and focus on meaning rather than decoding the text

Audiobooks are also a wonderful alternative to electronic games and DVDs, especially while traveling, and can be a valuable tool for winding down at bedtime. There are many wonderful book/tape or book/CD combinations available at libraries and bookstores, and many libraries now offer downloadable audiobooks as well. The American Library Association (ALA) has recently implemented a new award strictly for audiobooks—the Odyssey Award—covering choices from preschool through high school. They also provide annual lists of Notable Recordings for Children and Selected Audiobooks for Young Adults. Visit www.ala.org for more information.

> *"Fiction is like a spider's web, attached ever so lightly perhaps, but still attached to life at all four corners."*
>
> —Virginia Woolf

What to Read

This section contains age-appropriate reading recommendations for preschoolers:

As in the previous chapter, continue to provide . . .

- ✎ **Books with simple plots, several lines of text per page, and engaging illustrations.** Choose those about familiar subjects and activities, such as bathing, eating, sleeping, siblings, etc., as well as those about characters handling preschool emotions and experiences that children can relate to and retell in their own words.

- ✎ **Fairy tales** and books with animals or objects that think, talk, and behave like humans.

- ✎ **Rhyming or poetry books** that provide fun sounds and rhythms.

- ✎ **Books that invite physical exploration**, such as textures for touching, flaps to lift, tabs to pull, and holes to peek through or poke fingers in.

- ✎ **Homemade books and photo albums** with pictures of family members and friends.

- ✎ **Counting and ABC books** for continued skill-building.

In addition, look for . . .

Books that fuel your child's interests. Does your son or daughter love animals? Trucks? Princesses? Dinosaurs? Ballet? Providing books that speak to a child's personal passion is a powerful way to build on the association of reading with pleasure. It also affirms your child's individuality.

When our son Sam was very young, he was passionate about trucks. He only wanted to read stories (watch videos, wear T-shirts, play with toys) about trucks. Though I myself wasn't particularly interested in, let alone enamored by, trucks, I made an effort to find as many books as possible about them, since it was the only way to get Sam to read with me. We read truck book after truck book, ad nauseum. The more we read together, the more I (unwittingly) learned about trucks—and a funny thing began to happen.

Little by little, I began to appreciate trucks myself. Who knew there were so many kinds, or that so much in our world depended on the contributions they make to our lives? I began to appreciate their unique beauty, and the craftsmanship and skill it takes to design, build, and operate them. I began to stop and notice them on the street, even when Sam wasn't with me. Eventually, seeing a void in the truck genre fiction market, I co-wrote (with my Mom) a series of picture books, board books, and early readers about trucks (*Dumpy the Dump Truck*, Julie Andrews, Emma Walton Hamilton/Tony Walton) which were illustrated by my father, and which launched my professional writing career. Who would have guessed?

You may be surprised how many books exist that revolve around or celebrate your child's area of interest, both fiction and nonfiction. Ask your librarian or bookseller to help you conduct a search—or do one yourself. A word of caution, though: Be willing to read those same books a hundred times in a row . . . or to end up writing one yourself!

Reference books and support materials. The preschool years are a good time to introduce early dictionaries, encyclopedias, and other reference materials. In addition to helping with questions that may arise regarding words or subjects while reading, they also cultivate the habit of turning to these kinds of resources to learn more about a given topic or area of interest. There are many good "first" dictionaries and encyclopedias available for children, and exploring them together with your child at this stage will help them make better use of these important tools in later life.

> "The person who deserves most pity is the lonesome one on a rainy day who doesn't know how to read."
>
> —Benjamin Franklin

Junior science books. If your child loves learning how things work, or getting his or her hands into things, there are whole lines of books that celebrate that passion. From amusing fiction (*The Magic School Bus* series, by Joanna Cole and Bruce Degen, where a class of children takes trips with their eccentric teacher into space, the bottom of the sea, and even inside the human body, for instance) to ultra-readable educational books (like the *Let's Read and Find Out* science and nature series from Harper Collins), this could be just the way to engage and stimulate your budding scientist, inventor, physician, or mechanic in literary pursuits.

Wordless picture books that tell a complete story through illustrations only. Three of our favorites are:

- *Good Night, Gorilla* (Peggy Rathmann)
- *Good Dog, Carl* (Alexandra Day)
- *The Snowman* (Raymond Briggs)

Longer picture books and **short chapter books** that can last for several reading sessions.

Also…

Check out book/toy packages. While I'm somewhat reluctant to recommend materialism as a reading incentive, sometimes a well-chosen toy like *American Girl, Thomas the Tank Engine, Curious George*, etc. can engage a young person in a character's story.

American Girl is a case in point: The dolls are all based on characters from certain times in American history, and each comes packaged with a book that tells their "story." I have a dear friend and colleague whose daughter, now in third grade, has developed a passion for American history thanks to the American Girl series, and loves to read other books in the historical fiction and nonfiction genres.

Look for TV tie-ins. While it's essential that we do our best as parents to manage the hours our children spend in front of the "electronic babysitter," TV can have value when watched consciously and with parental involvement and guidance. In fact, it can become a reading ally when we purposefully seek out programs that have literary connections for our kids. Many children's television shows originated from books, such as:

- *Angelina Ballerina* (from the books by Katherine Holabird)
- *Arthur* (from Marc Brown)
- *Charlie and Lola* (from Lauren Child)
- *Clifford* (from Norman Bridwell)
- *Curious George* (from Margret and H.A Rey)
- *Franklin* (from Paulette Bourgeois/Brenda Clark)
- *Little Bear* (from Else Holmelund Minarik/Maurice Sendak)
- *Maisy* (from Lucy Cousins)

- *Max and Ruby* (from Rosemary Wells)
- *Rolie Polie Olie* (from William Joyce)

Many others offer a line of books in conjunction with the show, including:

- *Blue's Clues*
- *Caillou*
- *Dora the Explorer*
- *Little Einsteins*
- *Sesame Street*

Books that expand on your child's enjoyment of his favorite television characters can be a tool for reading enrichment, and can also serve to demonstrate the scope of books for children.

The Corporation for Public Broadcasting (CPB), along with PBS and the Ready to Learn Partnership, hosts a program called *Raising Readers* as part of their Ready to Learn initiative (http://pbskids.org/read/about.html). Through this initiative, they program literacy-based television shows for preschoolers, including *Reading Rainbow, WordWorld, Between the Lions, Super Why*, and, of course, *Sesame Street*, with many new "edutainment" shows in development for the coming years.

Needless to say, the real value in these shows is the degree to which you *participate* with your child in the learning. Though children certainly pick up a good deal just from watching the shows on their own, the value increases exponentially if you watch *with* them—and then extend the literacy concepts and ideas that the show introduces into your daily life.

And, for the reasons outlined on page 21 . . .

Continue to think beyond books! Magazines can make for entertaining reading with preschoolers. Choose those that have lots of pictures and speak to an area of interest—sports, animals, fashion—and see what ideas for stories you can find inside, or even make up from the pictures. The important thing is to spend time sitting with your children, turning pages, discussing what you find, and exploring and discovering the joy of reading together.

There are several magazines geared especially towards preschoolers, including:

- *Ladybug*
- *Click*
- *High Five*
- *Disney & Me*

Reading Techniques

You needn't give a full performance to engage your young audience in a story . . . but there are a few simple tricks of the trade that can go a long way toward inviting better listening skills and improving the experience for both of you. These tips have been separated into three groups: *Developing Listening/Critical Thinking Skills*; *Read-Aloud Skills*; and *Maximizing Interest*.

As always, the main principles to keep in mind when reading with kids are:

Invite participation. Encourage them to finish sentences—*"I'll huff, and I'll puff, and…?"*—and to provide sound effects, fill in the blanks, answer questions, point things out in illustrations, turn pages, act things out, etc.

Enlist other family members and loved ones—*especially* Dads and older siblings—to be "readers." Big brothers and sisters are great role models, and can be a huge asset here. But any beloved family member, caregiver, or friend who takes the time to share a story with your child will further reinforce the value and pleasure of reading. Remember—it's especially important for fathers to read with their children as much as possible. It bears repeating that the vast majority of preschool teachers are female, so it's vital—particularly for boys—to provide as much positive male role modeling as you can when it comes to reading.

> *"A book is a garden, an orchard, a storehouse, a party, a company by the way, a counselor, a multitude of counselors."*
>
> —Henry Ward Beecher

Accompany or follow the reading experience with a pleasurable, practical connection, whenever possible. For example, if you're reading *Bread and Jam for Frances* (Russell and Lillian Hoban), have some bread and jam ready for a nibble afterwards. This is especially effective when reading to groups of kids.

Developing Listening/Critical Thinking Skills

Offer your child something to play with or nibble on while reading. High-energy preschoolers may find it easier to listen to stories when their hands are occupied. If your child won't sit still for reading time, try offering crayons and paper, or a snack to calm and engage them while you read.

Stop from time to time to ask questions. Check in with your listeners regularly to gauge their comprehension of, and reactions to, the story. Invite them to make predictions as to where it might be going. *"Was that a good choice?" "What do you think is going to happen?" "Do you see what I see?" "Can you show me where the butterfly is?"*

Read-Aloud Skills

As discussed in the previous chapter, always try to:

- **Maintain color in your voice**—bring the story to life!
- **Point out and ask about things in the pictures**, inviting as much interactivity as possible.
- **Be consistently aware of your child's interest level**, and quit while you're ahead. Better to leave them wanting more!

In addition . . .

Introduce the book before you begin. Look at the cover together, read the title, author, and illustrator's name and talk about what the book might be about. You might also suggest things to listen or look for while reading the book.

Trace the lines with your finger as you're reading. This helps young children to follow along, and to begin to associate the letters, words, and images with the sounds they are hearing.

Slow down. One of the most common mistakes adults make when reading to kids is to read too fast. Take your *time*—let the ideas, the images, the richness of the language *land* on your listener before rushing ahead to the next sentence or page. Create an aura of suspense with a well-placed pause, or take a moment to share a "look" with your child—*"Isn't this exciting? I wonder what's going to happen next!"*

Try ending sentences with periods instead of question marks. A habit that many of us fall prey to is adding an upward inflection at the end of our sentences, or even at the end of a thought *within* a sentence.

This can take the form of an implied question mark—even if there isn't one in the punctuation—which is a habit many of us engage in as a means of inquiring whether the listener understands or agrees with what has just been said. It can also be an implied comma—a way of *leaning* into the next thought, or sentence, before the present one has been fully absorbed.

Both of these habits can make for a thin listening experience, in which the "meat" of the sentence or story is skimmed over rather than savored.

> *"Read in order to live."*
>
> —Gustave Flaubert

They also force the listener to do more work than necessary in terms of breaking out the ideas, images, or thoughts for themselves and experiencing each for its own merit.

Here's an example from *When We Were Very Young,* (A.A. Milne/Ernest H. Shepard):

> *"What is the matter with Mary Jane? She's perfectly well and she hasn't a pain, and it's lovely rice pudding for dinner again!"*

Experiment with reading this sentence using the punctuation as written, then trying it with an implied "period" at the end of each thought, so that each *modifies* or *builds* on the one before it:

> *"What is the matter with Mary Jane. She's perfectly well. And she hasn't a pain. And it's lovely rice pudding for dinner again!"*

Notice how the latter allows each thought, each image, to breathe, to stand by itself, before being modified by the next?

This is actually a professional acting technique and can take some practice, but once you get the hang of it, it becomes a new habit that strengthens your read-aloud skills and your speaking and communication abilities to boot.

Maximizing Interest

Use character voices or accents. Children love to hear the voices of individual characters come to life, and this can really activate a story and engage their imaginations. You don't have to ham it up too much—even a pitch change can make a difference in terms of establishing character—but if you *can* throw in a "voice" or an accent, so much the better.

Personalize the story. Incorporating your child's name into the text can be a great way for them to establish a personal connection with a story.

When our daughter Hope was born, we found a sweet board book called *Sam's Little Sister* (Yves Got). Since Hope's older brother is Sam, this was perfect, except for one thing—in the book, Sam's sister is named Sophie. I overcame this by typing the name "Hope" in a similar font to the one in the book and printing it out on small labels, which I then trimmed to size, peeled, and stuck over each reference to Sophie in the book. Suddenly, *Sam's Little Sister* was a very personal story about our two children—albeit in bunny form—and it is a book Hope has cherished ever since.

> "There is no mistaking a real book when one meets it. It is like falling in love."
>
> —Christopher Morley

A less literal—and elaborate—approach can be used with books that address the reader directly or only use pronouns. Try adding your child's name onto the end of a direct address sentence, or substituting it (or another name that's familiar or beloved) for pronouns or other character names in the book. For years, Arthur and D.W. in the wonderful series by Marc Brown had to be read as "Lisa" and "Lea" for Hope, who wants everyone to be female and has friends with those two names. She knew, of course, that the characters were really Arthur and D.W., but she loved the game and it made reading together all the more fun for her—although a little more of an exercise in concentration for *us*, since she busted us on every slipup!

Emma's Family Favorites for Preschoolers

"It is not enough to simply teach children to read; we have to give them something worth reading. Something that will stretch their imaginations – something that will help them make sense of their own lives and encourage them to reach out toward people whose lives are quite different from their own."

—**Katherine Paterson**

The preschool years are "golden time" in terms of reading with children. Specific interests and passions are beginning to emerge more clearly, and it's vitally important to take advantage of these in reading selections, as well as to be prepared to revisit favorites *often*. I cannot count the number of hours we spent reading truck books with Sam, and princess stories with Hope (I know, I know, painfully gender-obvious, but *their* choices!)—but the joy of hearing them "read" the same books quietly to themselves, almost verbatim, well before they could *actually* read, spurred us through any possible sense of tedium.

Many of the books on the **Babies and Toddlers** list remain favorites throughout this time. Below are some additional beloved titles:

Amy the Dancing Bear (Carly Simon/Margot Datz)
Singer-songwriter Carly Simon's book about Amy, a little bear who would rather dance the night away than sleep—and her exasperated mother, who is the one who ends up being tucked in.

***Angelina Ballerina* series** (Katherine Holabird/Helen Craig)
Angelina, the little mouse who lives to dance, has enchanted children for over twenty years. Spirited text and delightful illustrations—a bookshelf must.

Apples and Pumpkins (Anne Rockwell/Lizzy Rockwell)
The simple joys of Fall, from visiting a farm for apple- and pumpkin-picking, to carving Jack-o-lanterns and trick-or-treating.

Arthur series (Marc Brown)
Marc Brown's bestselling books (and Award-winning PBS-TV series) follow Arthur, the world's favorite aardvark, through daily life—losing a first tooth, getting glasses, going to camp, dealing with his feisty younger sister, D.W.—while delivering worthy and helpful life-lessons for youngsters.

> ***D.W.'s Guide to Preschool***—*Parents readying children for pre-school will be grateful: D.W.'s straightforward advice covers everything from bathroom breaks to snacks, naps, and center time.*

> ***D.W.'s Guide to Perfect Manners***—*D.W.'s brother, Arthur, dares her to be perfect for a day—can she smile, make her bed, and be agreeable all day, at home and school?*

Bad Dog, Marley! (John Grogan/Richard Cowdrey)
*Marley the dog is desperate to please, but always in trouble. Based on Grogan's bestselling **Marley & Me**, this picture book echoes the message that loving someone for who they are makes all the trouble worthwhile.*

Bark, George (Jules Feiffer)
The giddy tale of a puppy who speaks every other animal's language but his own—with superbly spare text and Feiffer's brilliant, classic line-drawings.

Bedtime for Frances (Russell Hoban/Garth Williams)
Frances, the irrepressible young badger, tries every delay tactic she can muster at bedtime. A perfect goodnight story for wide-eyed youngsters.

> ***Bread and Jam for Frances***—*After over-indulging in her favorite meal of bread and jam, Frances discovers that variety really is the spice of life.*

The Big, Big Sea (Martin Waddell)
The lyrical and beautifully illustrated tale of a mother-daughter jaunt to the sea, by the light of the full moon.

> **Owl Babies**—*Three worried owlets wait for their mother to return from her night flight.*

Charlie and Lola series (Lauren Child)
The hilarious brother/sister team from England (also a popular TV show). A series of delightful books celebrating the value of apologies, tomatoes, and the right shoes, to name but a few—all accompanied by Child's wonderful mixed-media artwork.

> **The Princess and the Pea**—*A terrifically funny twist on Andersen's familiar tale, featuring brilliant paper-doll princess illustrations against a photographic background.*

Corduroy (Don Freeman)
A stuffed bear in a department store finally gets adopted by the right girl. A childhood classic.

Don't Let the Pigeon Drive the Bus series (Mo Willems)
A brilliant tribute to the often dramatic and unreasonable behavior of preschoolers—with simple but hilarious illustrations. Get the whole series.

> **Knuffle Bunny** and **Knuffle Bunny Too**—*More of Mo Willems' comic genius, featuring the hilarious antics of a pre-schooler and her beloved stuffed bunny.*

Fancy Nancy series (Jane O'Connor/Robin Preiss-Glasser)
Glam-girl Nancy is determined to rescue her family from plainness by giving them lessons in the art of accessorizing.

Fire Truck (Peter Sis)
Little Matt imagines he is a fire truck—until a pancake breakfast brings him back to reality.

The Complete Book of the Flower Fairies (Cicely Mary Barker)
Cicely Mary Barker's classic rhymes and gorgeous illustrations celebrate every flower, tree, and bush—and its attendant fairy.

Frederick's Fables (Leo Lionni)
While the other mice busily prepare for winter, Frederick daydreams. But when winter sets in, it is Frederick's imagination that matters most. Lionni's fables celebrate timeless values and are accompanied by simple and evocative collage-style illustrations.

Froggy series (Jonathan London)
Scores of books in which Froggy starts school, learns to swim, acquires a sister, etc. The silly sound effects make this series is a great read-aloud.

The Golden Egg Book (Margaret Wise Brown/Leonard Weisgard)
Another classic tale about a bunny, and the new friend that hatches from a found egg.

>   **The Important Book**—*A book that encourages thought about the essence of everyday things.*

Grandfather Twilight (Barbara Helen Berger)
Grandfather Twilight takes his daily walk through the forest at day's end, to usher in the wonder of night.

Harold and the Purple Crayon (Crockett Johnson)
Harold takes a memorable journey with a simple purple crayon . . . First published in 1955, a tribute to the power and wonder of imagination.

If You Give a Mouse a Cookie series (Laura Joffe Numeroff/ Felicia Bond)
The first in the best-selling "If You Give a . . ." series. An enthusiastic mouse wears out an accommodating young boy with his demands— ultimately bringing everything back to square one.

I Love You Like Crazy Cakes (Rose A. Lewis/Jane Dyer)
The sweet story of an American mother and her new baby, adopted from China.

I Love You, Little One (Nancy Tafuri)
Seven young woodland creatures ask their mothers "Do you love me, Mama?" A quiet, lyrical book, providing assurance of the constancy of parental love.

***I Stink* series** (Jim and Kate McMullan)
A hilarious ode to the humble garbage truck, from the best-selling author-illustrator team. Other books in the series celebrate tugboats, dump trucks, etc.

Jazzbo Goes to School (Matt Novak)
School does not interest Jazzbo, until his mother finds just the right one.

Katy and the Big Snow (Virginia Burton)
A charming, old-fashioned tale about a little snowplow's courage and determination in the midst of a small-town blizzard.

> ***Mike Mulligan and His Steam Shovel***—*Mike Mulligan and his trusty steam shovel, Mary Anne, prove their worth in spite of modern technology in this touching tale about friendship and dedication.*

Lilly's Purple Plastic Purse (Kevin Henkes)
Lilly, the indomitable mouse, learns a valuable lesson about resolving conflict after she interrupts her class one too many times, in this wise and funny book.

> ***Lilly's Big Day***—*Lilly lobbies relentlessly to be the flower girl at her teacher Mr. Slinger's wedding.*

> ***Chrysanthemum***—*Chrysanthemum is proud of her name until she begins kindergarten. A tender and compassionate story about teasing.*

> ***Owen***—*Owen and his beloved blanket "Fuzzy" are inseparable, until the first day of kindergarten. Can his parents find a solution that suits everyone and helps their son transition?*

Make Way for Ducklings (Robert McCloskey)
Duck parents search for a safe place to raise their ducklings. A true classic, first published in 1941, with Caldecott-winning, sepia-toned illustrations.

Mole Music (David McPhail)
A sweet story about a violin-playing mole, reminding us that we never know the full effect of our actions—and of the power of music to change the world.

Miss Rumphius (Barbara Cooney)
A must-have for every child's library, this heartwarming story follows Alice Rumphius on her life's quest to see faraway places, live by the sea in old age, and do something to make the world a more beautiful place.

Mrs. McTats and Her Houseful of Cats (Alyssa Satin Capucilli/ Joan Rankin)
Subtle lessons in numbers and letters compliment this whimsical tale of Mrs. McTats and her 26 cats—plus one dog.

***Olivia* series** (Ian Falconer)
The "Eloise" of pigs! Ian Falconer's hilarious series about an unforgettable (if a tad precocious) porcine heroine.

The Paper Bag Princess (Robert Munsch)
A Prince and Princess slated to marry don't end up "happily ever after"—thank goodness, since the Prince is hopelessly shallow. A girl-power favorite.

> ***Thomas' Snowsuit****—Any parent who has met with a child's refusal to wear a snowsuit will relate to this story and envy those who live in Arizona.*

Pete's a Pizza (William Steig)
An amusing and endearing story about a father's attempts to cheer up his son on a rainy day by pretending to turn him into a pizza.

A Pig Named Perrier (Elizabeth Spurr)
A potbellied pig is missing something, despite his Hollywood life of luxury with his movie-star owner, until he takes a trip to a country farm.

Pinkalicious (Victoria Kann/Elizabeth Kann)
A little girl eats one too many pink cupcakes and turns pink for a day. . . . A book for pink-lovers everywhere.

The Snowy Day (Ezra Jack Keats)
The classic Caldecott Medal winner that pays homage to the wonder of a child's experience when the world is blanketed in snow.

> **Peter's Chair**—*A little boy wrestles with the arrival of his new sister, and her acquisition of all his "hand-me-down" baby things.*

Stella, Queen of the Snow (Marie-Louise Gay)
Stella responds to her little brother Sam's fears and boundless questions with a delightful blend of fact and fancy, encouraging him to share her joy in his first snowstorm. Others in the series include:

> **Stella, Fairy of the Forest**
>
> **Stella, Star of the Sea**
>
> **Stella, Princess of the Sky**

Sugarbush Spring (Marsha Wilson Chall/Jim Daly)
A warm and evocative story depicting life on a Minnesota farm at sap-collecting time.

Tell Me Something Happy Before I Go To Sleep (Joyce Dunbar/Debi Gliori)
Willoughby, a thoughtful bunny, calms his younger sister Willa's nighttime fears by encouraging her to think happy thoughts.

> **Tell Me What It's Like To Be Big**—*The sequel to "Tell Me Something Happy..." in which Willoughby reassures Willa that being big is something to look forward to.*

Toot and Puddle (Holly Hobbie)
The classic series featuring two good friends whose differing tastes celebrate being true to oneself while still being a true friend.

Where Is That Cat? (Carol Greene/Loretta Krupinski)
Miss Perkins has no intention of keeping the cat she has found, but each time a prospective owner comes by, the cat hides—and it soon becomes clear where "Fitz" will stay.

Winnie the Pooh (A.A. Milne/Ernest H. Shepard)
The "Bear of Very Little Brain" and his friends in the Hundred Acre Wood have delighted readers of all ages for over 80 years. A must for any library.

>**The House at Pooh Corner**—*in which we meet Tigger, and the adventures in the Hundred Acre Wood continue.*

>**When We Were Very Young** —*Milne's classic poems about the joys, complexities, and fantasies of childhood.*

>**Now We Are Six**—*More of Milne's gifted poetry about childhood, beloved by all ages.*

and *any* books by . . .

>Sandra Boynton
>
>Marc Brown (*Arthur* series)
>
>Margaret Wise Brown
>
>Eric Carle
>
>Lauren Child
>
>Kevin Henkes
>
>A. A. Milne
>
>Dr. Seuss

4

Elementary School:
Nurturing the Budding Reader

"Children's literature is our national potato... So many of the dreams and goals we have for our children, and that they have for themselves, can be advanced through the use of children's literature. So much of the blame exchanged between school, community, and family about education's failure can be converted into shared responsibility and success through children's literature. But the thing is, if you hand somebody a potato, or if you hand somebody a children's book, and he doesn't know how to cook... well, then."

**—Esmé Raji Codell, educator,
bestselling author and children's literature specialist**

There's absolutely no doubt that the elementary school years are a pivotal time for the development and consolidation of reading skills. Between kindergarten and fifth grade, not only are children learning to read independently, but their experiences during these years will have a major influence on their future relationship to books and to reading.

Here's the thing, though. As thrilling as it is to watch a child become an independent reader, it is absolutely *essential* that we, the proud parents, don't give ourselves a big pat on the back and *stop* reading to our children just because they're now able to read for themselves. But all too often, this is just what happens. According to the "Kids and Family Reading Report," a recent survey conducted by Scholastic, thirty-eight percent of children aged five to eight are read to daily (not a huge number in and of itself) ... but for nine to eleven year olds, this figure drops to just *twenty-three percent.*

No matter how easy our children's transition to independent reading is (but *especially* if it proves to be a challenge for them), it's vitally important that we continue to read with our children right through the elementary years—and beyond—in order to preserve and cement the association between reading and pleasure.

Reading together is also an important tool that can help children cope with the challenges of growing up. Stories about new siblings, visits to the hospital or the dentist, losing a pet, bullying, and social or cultural differences, for example, can open the door to important discussions about things that may be troubling children, and provide coping strategies as well as welcome reassurance during difficult times.

> "The secret at the heart of reading is the time it frees for the brain to have thoughts deeper than those that came before. The efficient reading brain quite literally has more time to think."
>
> —Maryanne Wolf,
> *Proust and the Squid*

A great way to strengthen the joy of reading when children are in their elementary years is to look for creative ways to support their emerging reading skills. Games and activities that provide subtle opportunities for them to practice their newfound skills in a fun way can help overcome any feelings of frustration they may be experiencing while they are learning to read independently. As their confidence grows, so too will their enjoyment and sense of empowerment.

As the great reading expert Jim Trelease says in his indispensable *The Read-Aloud Handbook*, "The more you read, the better you get at it; the better you get at it, the more you like it; and the more you like it, the more you do it."

Strengthening the Connections

The ideas that follow are designed to keep reading *inviting* to your child. The aim is to continually reinforce the connection between reading and pleasure, while at the same time sending subtle cues about the *value* of reading throughout our lives. You may wonder at times if these messages are getting through, but rest assured, they are—and they'll make a world of difference. Again, there are two overarching strategies:

1. Keep reading to—and with—your child. We've discussed this previously, but it is so fundamentally important that it's worth reiterating!

2. Set a good example! It's been said that one of the greatest gifts we can give our children is to show them what a happy adult looks like—and the fact is that parents who read regularly for pleasure are *six times* more likely to have kids who do the same.

In the Home

Continue to employ the approaches outlined in the previous chapters, including:

- ✎ **Provide a warm and inviting reading atmosphere**, being especially attentive to visual or noise distractions.

- ✎ **Cuddle while you read**—to reinforce the connection between reading and pleasure.

- ✎ **Build reading time into your daily routine**, at *least* once a day (but more is better!).

- ✎ **Maintain a "reading ritual"**—a gesture, expression, location, or action of some kind that is connected with the pleasure of reading and cultivates joyful anticipation as you begin.

- ✎ **Return to favorites as often as possible**, remembering the words of Daniel Pennac: "To re-read is to provide fresh proof of enduring love."

- ✎ **Keep letters and spelling games handy**—in the tub, on the refrigerator, as puzzles, etc.

- ✎ **Keep books *everywhere*.** A basket of books in the bathroom, kitchen, living room, playroom, and car ensures readiness for any reading opportunity that may arise, and makes a strong visual statement about the value of reading.

- ✎ **Be sensitive to timing with respect to choice of material**, staying away from darker or more challenging material at bedtime, for instance.

- ✎ **Create a "Book Nook" or "Reading Corner"** in your child's room or playroom to invite comfortable, well-lit, and cozy reading time.

- ✎ **Organize books attractively on shelves or in baskets**, to make favorites easier to find and send a visual message about respect for books.

- ✎ **Experiment with displays**, such as rotating selections that face out, or organizing according to size, genre, theme, etc.

- ✎ **Keep your child enrolled in a Book-of-the-Month club**, to help build his or her library and underscore the connection between books and pleasure

- ✎ **Surprise your child occasionally with an impromptu book gift**, to connect books with the joy of receiving affection.

and

- ✎ ***Never* withhold books or use them as a threat.** Words like *"If you don't behave, no before-bed reading tonight!"* turn books into weapons and create negative associations where you are trying to build positive ones.

In addition...

Allow—make that *encourage*—reading in bed. Allow kids to stay up late, as long as they're reading in bed. If they share a bedroom with others, give them a book light. Help them to discover the singular, sensual pleasure of reading in bed . . . and you will soon be hard-pressed to keep them from it.

One important caveat: Having a television or computer—especially one with Internet access—in your child's bedroom is a surefire way to bump reading way down the list of preferred bedtime activities. I'm a big believer in limiting televisions and computers to common rooms in the house, and keeping bedrooms as the sanctuary they should be. Our brains get bombarded all day long with electromagnetic frequencies—keeping them out of the bedroom to the fullest extent possible is a good way to equalize their effects, and helps us to sleep better and maintain better emotional and physical health to boot.

Beyond the Home

As described in detail in the previous chapters, continue to:

- ✎ **Visit libraries and bookstores as often as possible**, for all the unique sensory experiences that books provide. Inquire about

story hours, book-based activities, and visiting authors or
artists programs.

> *"Once started, the library is the biggest, blasted Cracker Jack factory in the world. The more you eat, the more you want!"*
>
> —Ray Bradbury

- ✎ **Encourage the giving of books as gifts** by grandparents and other family members and friends. (And make a big fuss about them when opened—thus underscoring their value for your child.)

- ✎ **Look for reading opportunities on outings**, while waiting for appointments, at the playground, etc.

- ✎ **Involve your child in performing and visual arts programs.** Students who actively participate in the arts are *twice* as likely to read for pleasure and three times more likely to win awards for academic achievement at school.

Actions and Activities

Here are some more practical activities designed to reinforce the joy and underscore the value of reading. Again, they have been divided into four areas: *Supporting Your Child; Encouraging Exploration; Skill Building;* and *Beyond the Home*, and again, let them serve as a springboard for creative ideas and activities of your own.

Remember, at the end of the day, the overarching aim of all these actions and activities is to:

Connect reading with life skills. Include your child in as many day-to-day activities that involve reading skills as possible—repairs and maintenance, grocery shopping, voting, etc.—and he or she will begin to experience the personal empowerment of reading firsthand.

Supporting Your Child

Keep up with the strategies described in the previous chapter, including:

- ✎ **Offer books as problem solvers**—Scores of wonderful, age-appropriate books abound on issues ranging from sibling rivalry, to bullying and peer pressure, to visiting the doctor.

Simply ask your local librarian or bookseller, or conduct a search on the subject matter on www.amazon.com or any other online bookseller.

↜ **Advocate for and support reading and literacy activities at school**, such as book fairs, author visits, book clubs, writers and illustrators weeks, book swaps, and reader's theater events. Encourage your school to participate in web-based programs, such as www.teachingbooks.net, which bring author visits into the classroom via the Internet.

↜ **Experiment with support activities** related to a favorite or current book.

For example, does your child enjoy Dr. Seuss's *The Cat in the Hat?*

Why not:

↜ Screen a movie version—either the original animated one, the more recent one starring Mike Myers, or an episode from the Jim Henson Productions' *The Wubbulous World of Dr. Seuss* series.

↜ Pick up a copy of the *Cat in the Hat Songbook*. Each silly song has a full piano score by Eugene Poddany, and many have simple guitar chords, too. You'll find songs that are "good for tongues, and necks and knees, of people, bees, and chimpanzees."

↜ Discuss rainy day activities and create a rainy day bulletin board or "Hat Full of Ideas" by having kids list their favorite things to do on rainy days.

↜ Attend a live performance of *Seussical: The Musical* which tours regularly across the country. (Visit www.theatreworksusa.org for more information.)

↜ Sing along with the original soundtracks of *Dr. Seuss's The Cat in the Hat* and *Seussical: The Musical*.

↜ Do an author study of Theodor Geisel (a.k.a. Dr. Seuss). Read his other books, study his biography, research him in an encyclopedia or online.

↜ Visit the Dr. Seuss National Memorial Sculpture Garden at the Springfield Museums in Springfield, Massachusetts. (www.catinthehat.org)

- Take a ride on the "Cat in the Hat Ride" at Seuss Landing, Islands of Adventure, Universal Studios.
- Play *Cat in The Hat* games online—visit www.seussville.com and www.randomhouse.com/seussville/games/concentration.
- Pick up a "Cat in the Hat" board game.
- Join a Dr. Seuss book club—through Scholastic's Beginning Readers Program, or start your own with family and friends.
- Create a Cat in the Hat edible hat:

  Ingredients: Round crackers or cookies, red Life Savers (gummy ones work best), white frosting

  1. Take one small round cracker or cookie
  2. Use a knife to spread a thin layer of frosting onto the cracker or cookie.
  3. Carefully place one red Life Savers in the middle of the cracker. This is the first red stripe on the hat!
  4. Spread more frosting onto the Life Savers.
  5. Add the second Life Savers.
  6. Spread more frosting.
  7. Top with the last Life Savers.
  8. Eat the cat's hat!

- Make wearable Cat Hats, with either red and white construction paper or felt.
- Make "Thing 1" and "Thing 2" T-shirts, using plain red T-shirts and white iron-on letters or transfers.
- Rewrite or retell the story from the cat's perspective.
- Have a cleanup relay race—set the timer for when "Mom will be home," don your cat hats, and set to it!
- Instead of "Duck, Duck, Goose" play "Cat, Cat, Hat."
- Write as many words as you can think of that have the letters "at" or create rhyming poems with "at" sounds.
- See how many (soft or unbreakable!) things you can balance at once.
- Eat cake in the bath.

The possibilities are limited only by your imagination. For more ideas, check out:

- *"Crafts from Your Favorite Fairy Tales"* (Kathy Ross)
- *"Story S-t-r-e-t-c-h-e-r-s: Activities to Expand Children's Favorite Books"* (Shirley C. Raines and Robert J. Canady)
- www.thebestkidsbooksite.com—"An Interactive Media Channel where Books, Crafts, Podcasts, Online Video and Web Resources Intersect"
- http://family.go.com/entertainment/pkg-crafts/—for craft ideas.

Or simply start by conducting an Internet search (using Google or any other search engine provider) on a beloved book or story title with your child, and see where it takes you. Ask your librarian for even more resources, and remember that most libraries have web access in addition to books, as well as someone to help navigate the web.

Encouraging Exploration

Continue to engage in the activities from the previous chapter, including:

- **Make up your own stories** while traveling, waiting for an appointment, etc.
- **Encourage your child to illustrate stories.** This is particularly effective, of course, when a book has not already been illustrated. My mother's book *The Last of the Really Great Whangdoodles* (Julie Andrews Edwards) is a case in point. Because the book is all about the power of the imagination, she chose not to have it illustrated so that readers would use their own imaginations to create images of the whangdoodle and other mythical characters for themselves. Needless to say, the countless renderings that she has received over the years from her young readers continue to warm her heart . . . and are a testament to the value of this idea.
- **Record yourself reading a favorite story** to create your own personal audiobook for your child.

⤹ **Play storytelling games with your child.** Here's a fun variation on this, especially if you've got a few family members or friends together:

> *Story, Story, Die!* (also known as "Conducted Storytelling")
>
> A storytelling game with its roots in improvisational theatre. One person is assigned to be the conductor, while the other players form a line facing the conductor. A title for a story, together with a genre or first line, is obtained from the audience or provided by the conductor. The conductor starts the game by pointing to a player, who immediately starts telling a story. At any point in time the conductor then points to another player, who has to immediately pick up and continue the story flawlessly, even if the switch happened in the middle of a sentence or word. Players that hesitate, or whose sentences are not grammatically correct or don't make sense, are booed out of the game by the audience yelling *"Story, story, die!"* The last player remaining gets to end the story and wins the game.

⤹ **Host story-time play dates or parties.** Structure play date or party activities (and goodie bags!) around a favorite book, or the theme of storytelling in general. For older kids, you might up the "fun" ante by telling or reading spooky stories around the fire, or by candlelight or flashlight.

⤹ **Write to your children!** Lunch or information notes, reminders, messages of affection, etc. If your child has an email address, by all means use it—but hand-written notes are important, too.

In addition . . .

Explore your family history, then create a family tree or write a biography together. This is a fun activity that strengthens literacy (and research) skills, while at the same time providing valuable family time. Help your child "interview" family members (grandparents can be especially helpful and willing in this regard), look up family records in local libraries and town archives, or simply take advantage of the many online genealogy services that exist today. Together you can create a genealogical chart, draw a family tree, or go as far as transcribing the interviews and compiling a book of your family's history, complete with photographs or illustrations. Take it a step further and publish it through one of the many print on demand services like www.lulu.com or www.iuniverse.com, and you have a wonderful and unique gift for family members of all ages. The same thing can be done with respect to the history of your house, street, neighborhood, or community.

> "It is not true that we have only one life to lead; if we can read, we can live as many more lives and as many kinds of lives as we wish."
>
> —S. I. Hayakawa

Engage in an author or illustrator study. Choose a favorite book, and then explore others by the same author or illustrator. Compare how their styles might change from book to book, or what signatures or trademarks identify them or make them so appealing. Find out more by visiting the author or illustrator's website or blog—most authors have one these days. Simply conduct an Internet search (using Google or any other search engine provider) on their name to find out whether they have a page of their own—if not, you can find out more about them from their publishers' websites, as well as from web articles. You might even go so far as to help your child pen a letter to a favorite author or illustrator, in care of their publisher. Writing can sometimes be a lonely business, and most authors love to hear from their readers. Some will even write back.

Skill Building

Continue to employ the strategies outlined in the previous chapter, including:

- **Tell stories about when *you* were a child**, to reinforce the idea that real life is full of stories.
- **Help your kids make their own books.** You can achieve this very simply and economically or quite professionally. See the previous chapter for specific recommendations on homemade books, book-making kits, and self-publishing and print-on-demand companies.
- **Play word games together.** From Scrabble® to Monopoly® to Trivial Pursuit®, board games of all kinds are important alternatives to television and electronic games. MadLibs® and

"homegrown" games like Hangman, Jotto and Essences are also fun ways to strengthen literacy skills while providing essential family time. Try one night a week TV-free, and play games together instead.

- ✎ **Cook with your child**, encouraging them to read and record the recipes with you, or perhaps even create a family recipe book.

- ✎ **Enlist your child's help with household chores.** Let them study the manuals or directions with you while assembling games or equipment, or making household repairs. Encourage them to read the list when out grocery shopping together, or the ingredients of a particular item. It's all about connecting reading with life skills in ways that are both pleasurable and inclusive.

In addition . . .

Encourage your kids to write their own stories . . . whether from their imaginations, inspired by other tales, or from events that they have recently experienced. And be sure to save them! My mother and I co-wrote the first draft of our picture book *Simeon's Gift* (Julie Andrews, Emma Walton Hamilton/Gennady Spririn) when I was in elementary school. Some thirty-something years later, we rewrote it, published it, then further developed it into a stage musical and then a symphonic event. You never know what might happen!

Promote journaling. Keeping a journal—during a family trip, for instance, or over a vacation—is another great way to engage kids in writing, and may interest them in reading other journalistic work. Journals can double as scrapbooks, and can be decorated by pieces of memorabilia, photos, drawings, etc. to make them more fun. Provide your child with some books that are told in journal format for inspiration, and invite them to choose the kind of journal they would be inspired to write in—leathery and grainy, bejeweled, with a lock, lined versus plain paper, etc.

Enlist your children's help in creating a year-end family newsletter. Using calendars, journals, datebooks, or photos, revisit the highlights of your year as a family together. Then ask your child to help craft the "story" to share with loved ones. You might include photos, or ask your child to contribute illustrations. This can become a cherished holiday ritual, and reinforces the idea that our daily lives are filled with stories.

Beyond the Home

Continue to pursue activities from the previous chapters, including:

- **See movies (or plays) based on books.** Whether the more recent efforts in this regard, such as:
  - *The Chronicles of Narnia* (from the books by C.S. Lewis)
  - *Harry Potter and the Sorcerer's Stone* (from J.K. Rowling's series)
  - *The Lord of the Rings* trilogy (from J.R.R. Tolkien)
  - *Shrek, Shrek 2*, and *Shrek the Third* (from William Steig)
  - *Holes* (from Louis Sachar)
  - *Bridge to Terabithia* (Katherine Paterson)

  or classics, like:

  - *Alice in Wonderland* (from Lewis Carroll)
  - *The Black Stallion* (from Walter Farley)
  - *Charlotte's Web* (from E.B. White, either the animated version or the more recent live-action one)
  - *Charlie and the Chocolate Factory* (from Roald Dahl)
  - *Cinderella* (from the Brothers Grimm)
  - *Freaky Friday* (from Mary Rodgers)
  - *The Little Mermaid* (from Hans Christian Andersen)
  - *Mary Poppins* (from P.L. Travers)
  - *The Miracle Worker* (from William Gibson)
  - *The 101 Dalmatians* (from Dodie Smith)
  - *Peter Pan* (from J.M. Barrie)
  - *Tarzan* (from Edgar Rice Burroughs)
  - *The Sword in the Stone* (from T.H. White's *The Once and Future King*)
  - *Treasure Island* (from Robert Louis Stevenson)
  - *The Wizard of Oz* and *The Wiz* (from Frank L. Baum)

  You can find out more about a particular film, including its cast, rating, and production information as well as interesting facts and trivia, by visiting the Internet Movie Database, www.imdb.com. And again, your local librarian can be a valuable resource in this regard as well.

↬ **Listen to audiobooks.** Research is showing that listening is just as effective as reading with the eyes, and suggests that audiobooks enhance fluency and comprehension. Libraries offer huge selections these days, whether to check out or download, and there are also a number of wonderful audiobook organizations, programs, websites and tools, many of which you will find in the **"Recommended Resources"** section at the back of this book. For instance, check out the new "Playaway" that many schools are using—self-contained audiobooks that look like iPods. Audiobooks make great choices when traveling, exercising, or in lieu of electronic games.

In addition…

Join (or start) a book club. Join a parent/child book club in your area, or start one of your own with family members or friends. Talking about a book with others and hearing each person's perspective on, or response to, a story can be a powerful way to cultivate a greater passion for reading. *The Kids' Book Club Book: Reading Ideas, Recipes, Activities, and Smart Tips for Organizing Terrific Kids' Book Clubs* (Judy Gelman, Vicki Levy Krupp) and *The Mother-Daughter Book Club: How Ten Busy Mothers and Daughters Came Together to Talk, Laugh and Learn Through Their Love of Reading* (Shireen Dodson) are both terrific resources for starting your own book club. Your local librarian or bookseller can also provide information about local book clubs or help in starting one.

Start a collection. Charms, buttons, postcards, coins, baseball cards, Beanies, Barbie, the Beatles, stamps, autographs … the possibilities for collections are endless, and books abound on all of them. Becoming a discerning collector might just motivate your son or daughter to read up on the subject … and you'll have a built-in gift-giving opportunity to boot. While we're at it, how about a *book* collection? Collect by author, genre, subject, style—or signed books, first editions, biographies, etc.

Experiment with "armchair travel." Take advantage of an upcoming (or recent) family trip, or that of another family member or friend. There are many wonderful children's books celebrating travel, both fiction and nonfiction, and a number that are specific to certain parts of the world. Miroslav Sasek's *This is . . . (London, Paris, etc.)* series for kids is a great place to start. Or . . .

- Trip to England? Read *The Wind in the Willows* (Kenneth Grahame), *The Secret Garden* (Frances Hodgson Burnett), or any of the *Paddington Bear* (Michael Bond) books.

- France? Try *Madeline* (Ludwig Bemelmans), *Anatole* (Eve Titus/Paul Galdone), *Little Bo in France* (Julie Andrews), or *The Invention of Hugo Cabret* (Brian Selznick).

- Italy? *Gaspard on Vacation* (Anne Gutman/Georg Hallensleben), *Gabriella's Song* (Candace Fleming/Giselle Potter), or *Zoe Sophia's Scrapbook: An Adventure in Venice* (Claudia Mauner/Elisa Smalley).

- Switzerland? *Heidi* (Johanna Spyri) or *William Tell* (Margaret Early).

- New York City? *Eloise* (Kay Thompson/Hilary Knight), *Lyle, Lyle Crocodile* (Bernard Waber), or *The Cricket in Times Square* (George Selden/Garth Williams).

You get the idea.

There are also terrific books that can tell you more about where many beloved children's stories take place. For example, Leonard Marcus's *Storied City: A Children's Book Walking-Tour Guide to New York City* features walking tours, maps, and photos celebrating over one hundred places in the city that inspired great children's books, such as those by Maurice Sendak, E.B. White, and Madeleine L'Engle, to name but a few. Joan Bodger's *How the Heather Looks: A Joyous Journey to the British Sources of Children's Books* describes the author's journey with her family through the back roads and villages of England to find the prototypes for places like Toad Hall and the Hundred Acre Wood.

You can also ask traveling family members or friends to send your kids postcards of their travels, and encourage kids to write and send their own.

One grandmother we know (who happens to also be a reading specialist) has taken this idea a good deal further. Being quite a globe-trotter in her retirement, she creates a homemade book for her grandchildren with stories and facts about every place she visits. Incorporating the photos she takes on her journey, she writes about what she has seen, whom she has met, and what the culture is like. Most of all, she writes about the *children* in the other countries—their schools, customs, diet, clothing, anything to engage her grandchildren's interest and imagination in reading about the new culture.

These lucky grandkids now have over a dozen spiral-bound and laminated books in their *Grandma Travels* series, ranging from *Grandma Hikes Coast to Coast in England* to *Grandma Treks and Travels in Thailand, Laos, Vietnam and Cambodia"* to *"Grandma Goes on Safari.*

Make a time capsule. This is a great way for kids to express their feelings and thoughts about their lives and their world to future generations. A time capsule need not be an elaborate metal cylinder embedded in the cornerstone of a building—it can be as simple as a shoebox full of carefully selected and archived items, reserved for opening until a later date. Here are some steps for creating a time capsule with your kids:

> *"A single book at the right time can change our views dramatically, give a quantum boost to our knowledge, help us construct a whole new outlook on the world and our life. Isn't it odd that we don't seek those experiences more systematically?"*
>
> —Steve Leveen,
> *The Little Guide to Your Well-Read Life*

1. **Choose the duration.** Do your kids plan to open the time capsule themselves, and if so when—in one year? Five years? Ten years? Would they like to share it with their own children or grandchildren? Would they like it to last long into the future?

2. **Decide where to store it.** Burying it may be fun, but it may also make the capsule more likely to be forgotten or lost, and much more susceptible to moisture damage. Also, bear in mind that you may move before the appointed time—so think about putting it where it can be readily found, but not in such a visible place as to be tempting to open ahead of schedule.

3. **Choose a container.** You can buy containers designed especially for time capsules, or use any waterproof, airtight, and preferably fireproof vessel. You might also consider using desiccant

gel bags, like those included in the packaging of electronic goods and in vitamin bottles. These help to absorb any moisture that may have been present at the time of encapsulation or that may find its way in down the line.

4. **Decide what will go in the capsule.** Start with a written description of what it is like to live right now. Encourage your kids to tell their future audience about their daily life—their feelings and activities, the latest trends, fashions, interests, and issues of concern. Have them mention favorite foods, music, books, movies, and hobbies. If possible, use acid-free paper. They can then choose to add things that reflect the present day, such as photos, newspaper or magazine clippings, price tags, coins, stamps, letters, arts and crafts, etc. Black-and-white photos last longer than color photos and will not fade as much, so use them whenever possible. You can also include CDs or DVDs, but if you plan to seal the capsule away for more than a generation, you should include instructions for using any equipment or recordings you include, as these items may very well be obsolete in the not too distant future.

5. **Protect the contents from decay.** Put everything into individual, airtight plastic bags. For extra protection, copy everything onto acid-free paper first. Leave out any substance that could decay and damage the other contents of the capsule, including rubber, wool, wood, PVC, and any perishable or edible item.

6. **Mark everything clearly**, so that the person opening it will know where each item came from and what its significance is. You might also include a detailed inventory of all the items.

7. **Seal the time capsule**, mark it with the date you intend for it to be opened, and stow, bury, or store it away in the intended place.

8. **Record the location of the time capsule and the date you intend it to be opened.** You might put a plaque or marker where you have hidden the time capsule, indicating where it can be found and when. Or, you can record the date and whereabouts in a journal, on a calendar, or in a family safety deposit box.

What to Read

Continue to incorporate…

- **Books that fuel your child's specific passions and interests**, i.e. stories about baseball, ballet, horses, etc.—both fiction and nonfiction.

- **Folk tales and fairy tales**, including those from other countries and cultures.

- **Poetry**—explore anthologies, as well as collections from one particular author.

- **Reference books**—The elementary years are an important time to take advantage of dictionaries, encyclopedias, and other reference materials. In addition to helping with questions that may arise regarding words or subjects while reading, they also cultivate the habit of turning to these resources to learn more about a given topic or area of interest—an important skill for lifelong learning.

- **Magazines**—There are many wonderful magazines geared especially towards young people these days. Some examples are:

3–6 Years

Ladybug

Click

Disney & Me

High Five

6–9 Years

Appleseeds

Ask

Highlights for Children

National Geographic Kids

Nick Magazine

Ranger Rick

Spider

Sports Illustrated Kids

Time for Kids

9–14 years

American Girl (8 to 12 years)

Calliope

Creative Kids

Cricket

Dig

Muse

National Geographic Kids

Sports Illustrated Kids

Time for Kids

You can also subscribe to "grown-up" magazines that speak to your child's passion: As a baseball lover, our Sam has long been a subscriber to *Yankees Magazine,* which he reads cover to cover. With all the statistics he studies, this has helped developed his math as well as his reading skills.

There are magazines for just about every passion on earth—riding, knitting, skateboarding, doll collecting—the list is endless. Find one that engages your child and you may be surprised by how much they read.

- ✑ **Science books**—Both fiction, like *The Magic School Bus* series (Joanna Cole/Bruce Degen), and nonfiction, like Harper Collins' *Let's Read and Find Out* series.

- ✑ **Book/toy (or game) packages**—such as American Girl, which provides a short historical fiction story with each doll character it sells.

- ✑ **TV tie-ins**—Try to connect your child's television viewing to reading whenever possible. Look for shows that either originated from books or that feature an accompanying book series (*Arthur* and *Charlie and Lola* are two good examples). You might also explore using the close-captioning option on the TV, with the volume turned low, to encourage "reading along."

In addition . . .

As children move through the elementary years, they quickly achieve new levels with respect to reading and listening skills. It's important to remember that *listening comprehension skills are usually several years ahead of reading skills,* so while your child's independent reading may still be limited to reading picture books or Early Readers, do keep stretching him or her with more challenging material when reading aloud, including longer picture books and chapter books.

Also include:

Books about characters handling elementary school emotions and experiences—siblings, starting school, losing teeth, etc. Elementary students especially appreciate humorous books about kids doing zany things (and learning from their experience, of course!).

"Series" books. Reluctant readers can often be hooked by a book series that takes familiar characters on new adventures. Popular choices for elementary students include:

- *The Magic Tree House* (Mary Pope Osborne)
- *Amelia Bedelia* (Peggy Parish)
- *Junie B. Jones* (Barbara Park)
- *Elephant and Piggie* (Mo Willems)
- *Clementine* (Sara Pennypacker)
- *The Boxcar Children*—Gertrude Chandler Warner
- *Nancy Drew*—Carolyn Keene
- *The Hardy Boys* (Franklin W. Dixon)
- and all those by Beverly Cleary (*Ramona the Pest, Henry Huggins, Ralph Mouse*)

. . . as well as picture book series like:

- *Arthur* (Marc Brown)
- *Olivia* (Ian Falconer)
- *Froggy* (Jonathan London and Frank Remkiewicz) and
- *Angelina Ballerina* (Katherine Holabird)

. . . to name just a few.

"How-To" Books. The myriad options in the "how-to" genre for kids range from very practical study guides on one topic of interest (such as *How Does the Show Go On: An Introduction to the Theater* by Thomas Schumacher and Jeff Kurtti) to broad overviews of multiple topics (such as *How To Be the Best at Everything* by Dominique Enright, Guy MacDonald, and Nikalas Catlow, who offer a boys' and girls' version). "How-to" books can often make for engaging reading when time does not allow for getting involved in a whole story—in the bathroom, for instance. Sam's current favorite in this regard is *The Encyclopedia of Immaturity—How to Never Grow Up* by the editors of Klutz. (Don't worry—it's not as terrifying as it sounds.)

Comic books and graphic novels. For reluctant readers, or those with reading challenges, these can often provide a portal to discovering the pleasure of books. The graphic novel is now a well-established genre that encompasses all ages, and the standards of excellence in the artwork and storytelling are compellingly high. Granted, some are of better value than others, but it is well worth researching which ones you endorse. (You might choose to avoid the more violent ones, for instance.) Some popular choices include:

- *American Born Chinese* (Gene Luen Yang)—winner of ALA's Michael Printz Award and finalist for the National Book Award
- *Babymouse* series (Jennifer and Matthew Holm)
- *Bone* series (Jeff Smith)

. . . and there are now graphic novel versions of popular novels, such as *Redwall* and *Artemis Fowl.*

One great resource to explore for further recommendations is *Sidekicks: A Website Reviewing Graphic Novels for Kids* (www.noflyingnotights.com/sidekicks/index.html).

Comic books can also be surprisingly engaging (and yes, they do constitute reading!). *Garfield* and *Calvin & Hobbes* are two popular series that kids from elementary through middle school enjoy, and there is now a new line called *Toon Books* (www.toon-books.com), which boasts the first high-quality comics designed for children ages four and up, vetted by educators and featuring original stories and characters created by veteran children's book authors, renowned cartoonists, and new talents.

Reading Techniques

Here are a few simple tricks of the trade that can go a long way toward inviting better listening skills and improving the read-aloud experience for both of you.

As always, the most important things to keep in mind when reading with children are:

- **Invite participation.** Make a special point to stop from time to time to ask questions, point out details, or invite your listener to make predictions.
- **Enlist other family members (especially *Dads*), friends, and older siblings to read aloud to the younger ones.** This takes the concept of "modeling" reading skills and belief in the value of reading and increases it exponentially. Dads who read with their kids significantly improve the chances of raising kids—especially boys—who read.
- **Accompany or follow the reading experience with a pleasurable, practical connection whenever possible.** For example, if you're reading *Cook-a-Doodle-Do* (Janet Stevens/Susan Stevens Crummel), have some strawberry shortcake ready to make and nosh on afterwards. This is especially effective when reading to groups of kids.

The following tips have been separated into three groups: ***Developing Listening/Critical Thinking Skills; Read-Aloud Skills;*** and tips for ***Maximizing Interest***.

Developing Listening / Critical Thinking Skills

Elementary students are ready to begin stretching their attention spans and listening skills, and these tips will greatly help to keep them engaged . . .

Stop from time to time to ask questions, such as *"What do you think is going to happen?" "Why do you think he did that?"* or *"What would you have done in that situation?"*

Relate a book to one you have read in the past. Draw parallels and make distinctions between plotlines, issues, writing styles, or character choices.

Follow up on a story. Look for opportunities throughout the day to make connections or draw parallels between something your child has read and real life. Comments like: *"This reminds me of that scene in the book when..."* and *"What a blustery day it is! Just like in Winnie the Pooh..."* or *"What do you think _____ might do in this situation?"* and *"How did you feel when _____ happened to Harry?"* provide openings for further dialogue and create important connections for young readers between reading and everyday life.

Read-Aloud Skills

Keep practicing the ideas from the previous chapters, including:

- **Set the stage before you begin.** If you're picking up where you left off from a previous reading experience, begin by discussing what you read yesterday and what might happen next. If it's a new book, begin by introducing the title, author, and illustrator, and by showing the cover.

- **Slow down.** Remember that young people's listening skills also involve a great deal of processing of new words and information. If you read at an adult clip, they may not be able to keep up. Don't read *so* slowly as to be labored or dull, but do pause for emphasis here and there, and take your time to "spin" the tale.

- **Maintain color in your voice.** Avoid monotones... try to enliven the experience for your listeners by employing a whisper here, emphasis there. Envision yourself as a storyteller, then play the role!

- **End sentences with periods instead of question marks.** Try to avoid upward inflections at the end of sentences, or *leaning* into the next sentence before the last has been fully absorbed. This can dramatically enrich the listening experience by allowing each thought to exist by itself before moving on to the next. (Re-read page 47 for details on this technique.)

Maximizing Interest

Continue to ...

Use character voices or accents to bring the individual characters in the story to life.

In addition . . .

Role-play with dialogue. Divide the character roles between you and your listener(s), and alternate reading the dialogue together. This is a great way to draw children into a story, and to help them learn to read aloud with expression.

Stop reading at a suspenseful point in the book. Try to leave your reader wanting more and looking forward to the next installment. To build further anticipation and excitement, find a moment or two in the day to say, *"I wonder what's going to happen next in . . ."* or *"Let's have our bath early tonight so we can be sure to finish our book!"*

Emma's Family Favorites for Elementary School

"What does someone just starting out in the world need to take? What book in his knapsack might help him along his way? (Not the one I've read today; it seems too nerve-racking, freighted with anxiety. It would weigh him down.) What builds courage? Lightens despair?"

—**Barbara Feinberg,**
Welcome to Lizard Motel: Children, Stories, and the Mystery of Making Things Up

The elementary years span a broad age-range, therefore the reading recommendations are equally diverse in scope. Most, if not all, of the **picture books** recommended in the preschool section are still beloved by this age group—as they now make great independent reads in addition to remaining favorite read-alouds. Also important at this stage are **Early Readers**, which generally come in series form. **Chapter books** are now ideal next-level read-alouds, and also make for more rewarding reading for older elementary students who may be ready for them.

Be sure to take advantage of the American Library Association's (ALA) annual lists of their award-winning books, as well as their Notable Children's and Young Adult book list (www.ala.org). You can also find great lists from **Reading Rockets** (www.readingrockets.org) as well as their new sister site, **AdLit** (www.adlit.org). For more ideas on finding great, age-appropriate books, see the **"Recommended Resources"** section at the back of this book.

Picture Books

Elizabeti's Doll (Stephanie Stuve-Bodeen/Christy Hale)
The Elizabeti series offers young readers a glimpse at the life of a child growing up in Tanzania. In this tender tale, Elizabeti longs for a doll, and creatively makes do with a stone instead.

Joan of Arc (Diane Stanley)
A magnificently illustrated picture book that marries history with compelling storytelling and artwork. Stanley's historical biographies cover a wide range of subjects, including Michelangelo, DaVinci, Shakespeare, and Queen Elizabeth.

Let's Read and Find Out **Science series** (various - *HarperCollins*)
Simple and direct concept-books that engage reader involvement with questions and answers coupled with lively illustrations. Personal favorites include:

> ***A Nest Full of Eggs*** (Priscilla Belz Jenkins/Lizzy Rockwell)
>
> ***From Caterpillar to Butterfly*** (Deborah Heiligman/Bari Weissman)
>
> ***How Do Birds Find Their Way?*** (Roma Gans/Paul Mirocha)
>
> ***Big Tracks, Little Tracks: Following Animal Prints*** (Millicent E. Selsam/Marlene Hill Donnelly)
>
> ***How a Seed Grows*** (Helene J. Jordan/Loretta Krupinski)

The Raft (Jim LaMarche)
A boy's lonely summer vacation is transformed by the discovery of a raft with animal figures painted all over it.

Skippyjon Jones **series** (Judy Schachner)
The hilarious antics of a hyperactive kitten, chock-full of rhyming chants and Spanish expressions.

The Sneetches and Other Stories (Dr. Seuss)
Four of Dr. Seuss's best-loved stories with important moral lessons.

> ***Horton Hears a Who!***—*The sweet, philosophical tale of Horton the elephant, who rescues a world on a speck of dust—because "a person's a person, no matter how small."*

Yertle the Turtle and Other Stories—*A trio of funny-bone-tickling tales with wise lessons contained within.*

I Had Trouble in Getting to Solla Sollew—*The comical tale of a journey to find a better place, which reminds us that troubles are better off faced than escaped.*

Oh, the Places You'll Go!—*The perfect send-off for children of all ages who are entering a new phase in their lives.*

The Stinky Cheese Man and Other Fairly Stupid Tales (Jon Scieszka)
Jon Scieszka, the first National Ambassador for Young People's Literature, is hilariously adept at fresh, irreverent takes on familiar tales. Among Jon's many other wonderful books are:

Math Curse

The True Story of the Three Little Pigs

The Frog Prince, Continued

Stone Soup (Jon J Muth)
The classic tale retold with Buddhist monks, who help a village discover the joy of sharing. Muth's vibrant watercolor illustrations are a delight.

Zen Shorts—*Short Buddhist tales integrated into a central story of three contemporary siblings who befriend a giant panda one rainy day.*

Zen Ties—*Muth's irresistible panda, Stillwater, and friends return in this tale of friendship, empathy, and the rewards of our emotional ties to one another.*

The Three Questions—*The gorgeous retelling of a Tolstoy tale, in which a boy asks three life-questions of a wise turtle, and learns the answers for himself.*

The Three Pigs (David Wiesner)
The familiar tale, redux—the three pigs leave the confines of their own storybook and enter into others. An amusing and thought-provoking poke at story structure.

Walter, the Farting Dog (William Kotzwinkle/Glenn Murray/Audrey Colman)
Trust me.

Where the River Begins (Thomas Locker)
A boy and his grandfather journey into the mountains to find the source of water. Accompanied by Locker's glorious landscape paintings.

I Can Read / Early Readers

One of the great things about Early Readers is they tend to come in series format, such as . . .

Amelia Bedelia (Peggy Parish)
The hijinx of a beloved but literal-minded housekeeper.

Biscuit (Alyssa Satin Capucilli)
The adventures of an adorable pup and the little girl who loves him.

Cowgirl Kate and Cocoa (Erica Silverman/Betsy Lewin)
A young cowgirl and her talking horse.

Frog and Toad (Arnold Lobel)
Two best friends, always there for each other.

Henry and Mudge (Cynthia Rylant and Suçie Stevenson/Carolyn Bracken)
The escapades of young Henry and his gigantic, beloved mastiff.

Little Bear (Else Holmelund Minarik/Maurice Sendak)
The first "I Can Read" series, celebrating the simple family values of Little Bear, his family, and his friends in the woods.

Mercy Watson (Kate Dicamillo/Chris Van Dusen)
The hilarious hijinks of a porcine wonder.

Poppleton (Cynthia Rylant/Mark Teague)
Tales of a city pig who moves to the country.

Tales of Amanda Pig (Jean Van Leeuwen/Ann Schweninger)
A wholesome collection of stories about how Amanda handles everyday life, and how her parents, in turn, handle her.

Chapter Books

The BFG (Roald Dahl)
A young orphan is kidnapped by a "BFG"—that's "Big Friendly Giant"—and taken off to the Land of the Giants. One of Dahl's best-loved works.

The Borrowers series (Mary Norton)
A multi-award-winning classic, featuring a magical world of tiny people who live underneath the floorboards of an English country home and borrow all manner of objects from above. Other titles in the series include:

> **The Borrowers Afield**
>
> **The Borrowers Aloft**
>
> **The Borrowers Avenged**
>
> **The Borrowers Afloat**

Bridget (Gen LeRoy)
Bridget makes increasingly zany attempts to get the boy she likes to notice her.

> **Emma's Dilemma**—*Emma's asthmatic grandmother moves in, which means the beloved family dog must move out.*

Charlie and the Chocolate Factory (Roald Dahl)
Only five children will be allowed inside Willy Wonka's new chocolate factory—but they're in for the adventure of a lifetime.

Clementine series (Sara Pennypacker)
A spirited third-grader, with a knack for trouble and a big heart.

The Cricket in Times Square (George Selden)
The adventures of a musical country cricket, accidentally transported to Times Square.

D'Aulaire's Book of Greek Myths (Ingri D'Aulaire/Edgar Parin D'Aulaire)
The best-loved children's book about the gods and goddesses, kings, and heroes of ancient Greek mythology.

Frindle (Andrew Clements)
A 5th grade boy coins a new word for "pen"—and soon the whole country is using it!

From the Mixed-Up Files of Mrs. Basil E. Frankweiler (E.L. Konigsburg)
Claudia decides to run away from home with her younger brother, and chooses to live in the "comforts" of the Metropolitan Museum.

Harriet the Spy (Louise Fitzhugh)
Aspiring writer Harriet spies on her friends and records her notes in a notebook—but her world is turned upside down when the notebook is discovered.

The Hundred Dresses (Eleanor Estes)
A powerful book about the pain of being teased at school, and one girl's journey to compassion.

The King's Equal (Katherine Paterson)
A prince searches for his equal in beauty, intelligence, and stature— and finds her, and his humility, in a simple country girl.

The Last of the Really Great Whangdoodles (Julie Andrews)
Three children and an eccentric professor of genetics travel to "Whangdoodleland" to rescue the last mythical creature from potential oblivion.

The Magic Tree House series (Mary Pope Osborne)
Jack and Annie have countless adventures, traveling through time and space, thanks to a magic tree house.

Mandy (Julie Andrews)
A young orphan finds her purpose—and eventually her family—by restoring an abandoned shell cottage and its garden.

Misty of Chincoteague series (Marguerite Henry)
The classic series based on the real-life wild ponies from the island of Chincoteague. Other titles include:

> **Stormy, Misty's Foal**
>
> **Sea Star: Orphan of Chincoteague**

Misty's Twilight—... *and there are scores of Henry's other horse tales beyond the "Misty" series.*

Mr. Popper's Penguins (Richard and Florence Atwater)
The delightful tale of Mr. Popper the house-painter and his houseful of penguins, ice rink included.

My Father's Dragon (Ruth Stiles Gannett)
A boy named Elmer rescues an over-worked and under-appreciated baby flying dragon. The sequels are great, too:

Elmer and the Dragon

The Dragons of Blueland

Pippi Longstocking series (Astrid Lindgren)
The irrepressible, pig-tailed hero who lives alone with her pet monkey and whose high-spirited adventures cause as much trouble as fun. Others in the series include:

Pippi in the South Seas

Pippi Goes on Board

Pippi Goes to the Circus

Pippi's Extraordinary Ordinary Day

Ramona series (Beverly Cleary)
Beverly Cleary's books have delighted generations, and Ramona "the Pest" Quimby, age 8, is one of her best-loved characters. Titles in the series include:

Ramona the Brave

Ramona and Her Father

Ramona and Her Mother

Beezus and Ramona

Ramona the Pest

Ramona Forever

Ramona's World

Ramona Quimby, Age 8

Cleary also wrote a series about Ramona's neighbor, Henry, and his dog, Ribsy, who get up to all kinds of shenanigans together, including:

Henry Huggins

Ribsy

Henry and Ribsy

Henry and Beezus

Henry and the Paper Route

Henry and the Clubhouse

The Secret Garden (Frances Hodgson Burnett)
A Victorian orphan and her sickly cousin discover a new appreciation for life through the care of a secret garden. A childhood classic.

Stuart Little (E.B. White/Garth Williams)
The famous mouse, born to a family of people who set out on a quest across the American countryside. A classic.

Charlotte's Web — The timeless tale of friendship between Wilbur the pig and a spider named Charlotte.

The Trumpet of the Swan — Louis the swan has no voice — but communicates with a trumpet, and eventually by reading and writing, thereby winning his lady's love.

5

Middle School and Beyond: Deepening the Roots

"Properly, we should read for power. Man reading should be man intensely alive. The book should be a ball of light in one's hand."

—**Ezra Pound, Poet**

The middle school years are an especially vulnerable time for reading. When our son Sam entered fifth grade, he was an enthusiastic reader. The cultural history program that forms the basis of his school's curriculum was focused that year on emerging civilizations, from tribal associations to more complex forms of social and political organization and, as such, it featured a heavy emphasis on war and death. Since integrated learning is the foundation of the school's pedagogy, these topics were then reflected in the books being assigned. Sam is a sensitive kid with a big heart, and as the year progressed, we began to notice him reading with less and less enthusiasm. He complained that the books were "depressing" or "scary," and he often suffered bad dreams, sleeplessness, and anxiety. We wondered how much of this might be related to the subject matter he was being asked to wrestle with—including graphic violence, children (and parents) dying, and the ravages of war.

I shared my concern with a reading-specialist friend and teacher, and she referred me to an extraordinary article by Barbara Feinberg called "Reflections on the 'Problem Novel'—Do These Calamity-Filled Books Serve Up Too Much, Too Often, Too Early?" adapted from her book *Welcome to Lizard Motel: Children, Stories, and the Mystery of*

Making Things Up. This courageous piece of writing posits that, awards and endorsements notwithstanding, much of today's "recommended reading" for middle and high schoolers is "something akin to a 'good beating', to make our children better, build character."

"Realistic fiction," or "problem-centered books" as they are sometimes called, can certainly help many children develop the courage to face the challenges in their own lives. At some point, we have all experienced the kind of restored perspective that comes from realizing how much better off we are compared to the next guy.

But for some kids—and our Sam is one—this kind of reading actually serves to instill deep anxiety, and even a kind of dread . . . not only of reading, but of growing up. Feinberg's article closed with an insight that moved me deeply:

> *"I have realized what is missing in those books: Open destiny.*
>
> *It's from a line in a Grace Paley story. She describes how she hates stories that move from point a to point b, toward an ending that's fixed before starting out. You know, contrived. She says she hates that absolute line between two points . . . not for literary reasons, she says, but because it takes all hope away. 'Everyone, real or invented, deserves the open destiny of life.'"*

I reached out to Sam's teacher, conveying respect but also concern, and expressing my hope that the year might also include some more joyful fare to maintain our developing reader's enthusiasm. She understood (though perhaps thought I was babying Sam just a bit), but as the curriculum had been established and the reading choices committed to by the school, there wasn't much she could do.

> "We shouldn't teach great books; we should teach a love of reading."
>
> —B.F. Skinner

So we began to work more diligently on counterbalancing the darker stuff with home-based reading that had some levity and playfulness. We also focused on making sure we were in touch with what Sam was reading ourselves. In this way, his father and I could have meaningful conversations with him about areas of concern as they arose. I'm happy to report that, as I write, Sam is back to being an enthusiastic reader . . . and sleeping better, too.

The key to negotiating the middle and high school years, I feel, is to stay in touch with our kids. Of course, we must trust our pre-teens and teenagers—we must begin to empower them and let them test their wings—but as best we can, we must also continue to let them know we are there, that we care, and that we understand and support who they are.

And we must be *vigilant* about protecting the joy, the gift—the *open destiny*—that reading can provide for their future.

Cementing the Connections

The ideas that follow focus on keeping reading *inviting* as your child grows older and is presented with more life options. As always, the aim is to continuously, subliminally reinforce the connections between reading and pleasure, while at the same time sending subtle cues about the personal empowerment that comes from reading. As before, there are two key strategies:

> *"The single most important activity for building the knowledge required for eventual success in reading is reading aloud to children. It is a practice that should continue through the grades."*
>
> —Commission on Reading, (National Academy of Education, National Institute of Education, and U.S. Dept. of Education) *Becoming a Nation of Readers*

1. **Keep reading with your child.** Really. Continue reading aloud to your older child, wherever and whenever possible. It isn't until around eighth grade that young people's reading abilities and listening skills *converge*—meaning that until that point, children can understand a great deal more of what is read *to* them than they are able to read to themselves, both in terms of vocabulary *and* ideas. This alone should be incentive enough to continue reading aloud with kids through middle-school. But there's also the fact that continuing to read together through the middle school years keeps the connection between reading and pleasure alive, as well as helping young people to become better readers themselves and discover what kinds of stories and authors inspire them. Plus, it provides important opportunities for you to explore social and moral issues together.

You may be surprised by how receptive your middle schooler is to being read to . . . but if he or she finds it embarrassing or babyish to be read to, then try inviting them to do the reading—to you, to a younger sibling, or to a relative or friend, perhaps. If you have children of diverse ages, you can look for books that span generations to read aloud, ostensibly to the younger one, but in a time and place that your older child can listen to and benefit from as well. If your older child is *truly* resistant, check the further recommendations for reading aloud with older kids in the **"Frequently Asked Questions"** section at the end of this book.

2. **Keep setting a good example!** Continue to provide the visual cue, and emotional message, that reading is an important and enjoyable lifelong activity.

In the Home

As described in the previous chapters, continue to . . .

- ✑ **Provide a warm and inviting reading atmosphere**, supported by comfortable seating and good (not harsh!) lighting, and free of noise or visual distractions.

- ✑ **Snuggle up together while you read.** Middle schoolers who have grown too big for laps often miss snuggling with their parents and loved ones. Their bodies are approaching adulthood, but their hearts and minds are still those of a child. Snuggling together is a powerful kinesthetic way to reinforce the association between reading and warmth, joy, and love. Be creative about looking for ways to express your affection while you read with your older child. Even just letting them rest their head or feet in your lap can send a powerful message.

> *"After all manner of professors have done their best for us, the place we get knowledge is in books. The true university of these days is a collection of books."*
>
> —Thomas Carlyle

- ✑ **Keep books everywhere**—in addition to bookshelves in bedrooms, playrooms, and libraries, the "well-read house" should include baskets or totes in the bathroom, kitchen, living room, den, and car... always available, and always making a visual statement about the value of books in our lives.

- **Ensure that an inviting "Book Nook" or "Reading Corner" is available.** Designate a corner of your child's room as the reading area, and help them set it up and decorate it in an inviting way—good lighting, comfy chair or beanbag, soft pillows, a small table for drinks or snacks.

- **Keep your child enrolled in a Book-of-the-Month club**, to expand his or her library and maintain the connection between books and joy.

- **Surprise your child occasionally with an impromptu book gift**, to connect books with the joy of receiving affection.

- ***Never* withhold books or use them as a threat.** Be mindful not say things like, *"If you don't ___, no reading time tonight!"* This turns books into weapons, and quickly creates negative associations where you are trying to build positive ones.

- **Encourage reading in bed**, but don't forget the caveat about televisions—and computers—in the bedroom, as mentioned on page 60.

In addition...

Help your child keep his or her books well organized. This demonstrates respect for them, and makes it much easier to find the "one" he or she may be looking for at any given moment. Cluttered piles send a negative message—and can undermine your child's best efforts if he or she is unable to find a sought-out book within a reasonable amount of time.

Be mindful, however, not to turn shelf maintenance into such a chore that your child begins to develop a negative association with books... it's all about balance.

Beyond the Home

Continue to employ the strategies detailed in the previous chapters, including:

- **Visit libraries and bookstores together as often as possible.** Ordering books online may be simpler, but nothing beats a visit to a *real* bookstore or library. Attend visiting authors or artists programs and book signings. Encourage your child to participate in the library's summer reading program and/or book clubs. Remember, libraries are *free!*

- ☞ **Encourage the giving of books as gifts** by grandparents and other family members and friends.

- ☞ **Recommend (or provide) reading selections for outings**, while waiting for an appointment, for instance, as an alternative to the iPod or electronic games.

- ☞ **Involve your child in performing and visual arts programs.** Middle schoolers are perfectly suited, age-wise, for attending plays, reading scripts, and discussing performances, as well as for attending arts camps, clubs, and other programs. Remember—young people who actively participate in the arts are *twice* as likely to read for pleasure as those who do not, and *three* times more likely to excel at school!

Actions and Activities

The following activities have been divided into four areas: ***Supporting Your Child; Encouraging Exploration; Skill Building;*** and ***Beyond the Home***. Again, try as many as you like, and let them act as a springboard for coming up with more creative ideas and activities of your own.

> *"Everything you need for a better future and success has already been written. And guess what? All you have to do is go to the library."*
>
> —Jim Rohn

As before, the overarching aim of all these actions and activities is to connect reading with life skills. Consistently show (rather than *tell*) your pre-teen or teenager how many ways in which reading skills empower our lives by involving him or her in as many day-to-day activities that entail reading as possible—such as repairs and maintenance, grocery shopping, and voting.

Supporting Your Child

As in the previous chapters, it is important to continue to . . .

- ☞ **Offer books as problem solvers.** A well-written and well-timed book that addresses an issue your child is wrestling with can be a godsend to you both. "Bibliotherapy" offers reassurance to your child that he or she is not alone, and can provide new ideas for coping strategies as well as some comic relief. It also teaches your child to turn to books for answers to questions or problems in later life.

From peer pressure to divorce to sibling rivalry, the topics that classic children's literature covers are limitless. Simply ask your local librarian or bookseller, or conduct a search on the subject matter on www.amazon.com or any other online bookseller. If your older child balks at something that feels "imposed" upon them by Mom or Dad, try leaving a book casually in their room or bathroom, where they can happen upon it without fear of embarrassment.

✍ **Deepen reading experiences with support activities.** Look for activities that build on and support the ideas or themes within a favorite book. Bake a recipe, build a model, play a game, visit a place mentioned in a book, or attend a relevant museum exhibit. Find music, watch a TV program, or see a movie that expands on a theme or topic.

For example, is your child reading *The Lion, the Witch and the Wardrobe* from C.S. Lewis's *The Chronicles of Narnia*?

Then why not:

✍ Screen one or more of the film versions (for older kids, you might include the poignant film *Shadowlands,* which chronicles the story of Lewis's marriage).

✍ Read all the books in *The Chronicles of Narnia* series, as well as other works by Lewis—including his poetry and essays.

✍ Conduct a C.S. Lewis author study.

✍ Visit some of the many websites celebrating the author and his books, including www.cslewis.org, "Into the Wardrobe" (http://cslewis.drzeus.net), www.narniaweb.com, and www.thelionscall.com

✍ Pick up a copy of *The Narnia Cookbook*, by Douglas Gresham, Lewis's stepson, and experiment with some of the many recipes inspired by the books.

✍ Delve into the photo-biography *C. S. Lewis: Images of His World* by Douglas R. Gilbert and Clyde S. Kilby.

- Explore some of C.S. Lewis' influences and passions—the Icelandic Sagas, Norse, Greek and Irish mythology, and the works of J.R.R. Tolkien (his friend and colleague at Oxford), as well as W.B. Yeats and Beatrix Potter.

- Visit *The Chronicles of Narnia: International Museum Exhibition,* a state-of-the-art educational exhibit premiering in 2008 and scheduled to appear at internationally renowned museums and learning institutions in a minimum of 10 cities around the world over a five-year span.

- If you're planning a trip to the U.K., pick up a copy of *Touring C.S. Lewis' Ireland & England* by Perry C. Bramlett and Ronald W. Higdon, and *A Guide to the C.S. Lewis Tour in Oxford* by Ronald K. Brind. Then, take the tours!

- Sample assorted flavors of Turkish Delight—you can buy it pre-made or find recipes to make your own.

- Listen to the soundtracks from the various Narnia films, as well as *The Roar of Love: A Musical Journey into the Wonder of C.S. Lewis' Narnia* by 2nd Chapter of Acts and various *Music Inspired by The Chronicles of Narnia* CDs.

- Play a Narnia board game, puzzle, or computer, video, or online game.

- Do a study of Narnia art—numerous artists and illustrators have crafted their own versions of the world and its characters.

Advocate for and support reading and literacy activities at school. Schools can provide wonderful enrichment opportunities when it comes to reading, and many publishers offer teachers guides, book clubs, and other resources for use in the classroom, and can assist in securing author or illustrator visits. Encourage your school to participate in web-based literacy programs or to host a "Big Read" or "One Book One School" event. (http://www.loc.gov/loc/cfbook/onebook/)

It's also vital that parents advocate for library funding, not only for books but also for proper staffing as well as media centers. Many schools across the country have experienced cutbacks in these areas, but fortunately grassroots organizations have begun to have an impact on restoring federal funding and can make a huge difference. Visit www.ilovelibraries.org to learn more and get involved.

In addition…

Get familiar with what your child is reading at school. I know, I know. With all the responsibilities, challenges, and chores associated with parenting teenagers, couldn't we just trust the schools on this one? Surely if the book assigned this month has won such-and-such a medal, it must be valuable reading? Maybe. But it depends on your kid. (This is the flipside of the previous strategy, by the way!)

As I described at the beginning of this chapter, a lot of what's out there in children's literature these days is pretty challenging stuff and can affect our kids in myriad ways. I'm certainly not advocating censorship, or even conservatism—I'm just saying, know your children and stay in touch. At the very least, you'll be better equipped to have a meaningful dialogue with them about some of the subjects that they are dealing with, and able to find "teachable moments." And at best, you may be able to fend off the kind of shutdown that can result from one depressing, boring, or disturbing reading experience too many.

Set goals and offer rewards. It's true that as children become more proficient at reading, they are better able to enjoy its pleasures—and it is with this in mind that I cautiously recommend the reward system for a book (or chapter) finished. Remember that a goals/rewards system need not be materialistic in approach—something like allowing a child to stay up late as long as he or she is reading can often be enough incentive to produce results. Or try something related to reading, such as a gift card for the bookstore, bookmarks, or pencils. Take care, however, that the spirit in which this is engaged is one of building incentive and connecting reading with fun . . . and be ready to change your strategy if at any point the pressure of the goal threatens to cross over into an association with frustration.

Encouraging Exploration

Continue to employ those strategies from the previous chapters that feel age-appropriate, including:

- **Write to your children!** Notes, reminders, messages of affection, emails—use text to communicate with your child whenever possible. Write letters or emails when you have to be apart for any length of time, or just to engage in a dialogue about something. Not as a substitute for real-life dialogue, of course, but as a supplement . . . sometimes we can convey feelings or reason more clearly and effectively in print.

- **Explore your family, home, or community history, then create a family tree, chart, or biography together.** Encourage your child to interview family or community members, look up records in local libraries and town archives, or take advantage of an online genealogy service. Ellis Island has a wonderful online free resource to find out what ship family members came over on (www.ellisisland.org). If you register (free) you can even see a photo of the ship. Then create a genealogical chart or family tree together—or compile a family biography, complete with photographs or illustrations. Publish it through one of the many affordable print-on-demand services like www.lulu.com or www.iuniverse.com, and you have a wonderful and unique gift for family members of all ages.

- **Engage in an author or illustrator study.** Explore several books by the same author or illustrator, noting any changes, signatures, or trademarks in their writing style. Visit an author or illustrator's website or blog—or find out more from their publishers' websites and from web articles. You can write to a favorite author or illustrator in care of their publisher. Most authors love to hear from their readers—and some will even write back.

Skill Building

- **Play storytelling and word-based games as a family.** Re-read the entry on "Story, Story, Die!"—also known as "Conducted Storytelling," which is a great game with older kids (page 65). Games like Scrabble are obviously terrific for strengthening reading (and spelling) skills, but there are many other great board games that provide skill-building opportunities while strengthening the correlation between reading and fun. MadLibs and "homegrown" games like Charades, Jotto, Essences, Bartlett's, and Dictionary are also wonderful ways to strengthen literacy skills while providing meaningful family time.

In our family we often play games when we are on holiday or at a family gathering. One we particularly enjoy is:

- ✐ **"The Three Minute Game"**—Everyone writes a topic on a piece of paper . . . anything from "penguins" to "the person on my left." All the topics go into a hat, and each player selects one. With a moderator timing, all players have three minutes to write—quickly, free-association style — on their selected topic. When the time is up, the moderator can read all the entries aloud anonymously, or each person can read his or her own. This is a simple, non-competitive game that can be both hilariously funny and surprisingly revealing.

- ✐ **Encourage your kids to write their own books and stories** . . . and be sure to save them! Christopher Paolini wrote the first draft of his bestseller *Eragon (The Inheritance Series)*—later made into a feature film— when he was just fifteen years old. You never know what might happen!

> "Only a generation of readers will span a generation of writers."
>
> —Steven Spielberg

- ✐ **Help them publish their own books.** With the new trends in self-publishing and print on demand (POD), there are a number of companies that will actually publish your children's work, at varying levels of cost. A few to explore are www.outskirtspress.com, www.lulu.com, www.xlibris.com, www.iuniverse.com, and www.authorhouse.com.

- ✐ **Cook together**, encouraging your kids to read and record recipes with you, and create family recipe books.

- ✐ **Enlist their help with household chores.** Have your kids read the manuals or directions to you while assembling games and equipment or making household repairs, read the list when out grocery shopping together, or the directions to a destination on a map. Aim for connecting reading with life skills in a way that is both pleasurable and inclusive. Be sure to take your kids with you when you vote!

- ✐ **Promote journaling or scrapbooking**, during a family trip, over a vacation, or anytime.

೮ **Create a year-end family newsletter together**, to share with loved ones. This can become a cherished holiday ritual, and reinforces the idea that our daily lives are filled with stories.

Beyond the Home

Continue to pursue the strategies outlined in the previous chapter, including:

೮ **See movies (or plays) based on books.** Include the more recent efforts in this regard, such as:

- *The Chronicles of Narnia* (from the original books by C.S. Lewis)
- The *Harry Potter* films (from J.K. Rowling's series)
- *The Lord of the Rings Trilogy* (from J.R.R. Tolkien)
- *The Golden Compass* (from Philip Pullman)

. . . but don't forget classics, like:

- *1984* (from George Orwell)
- *The Color Purple* (from Alice Walker)
- *Dracula* (several versions— from Bram Stoker)
- *Frankenstein* (from Mary Shelley)
- *Gone with the Wind* (from Margaret Mitchell)
- *The Grapes of Wrath* (from John Steinbeck)
- *Great Expectations* (from Charles Dickens)
- *Little Women* (from Louisa May Alcott)
- *The Miracle Worker* (from William Gibson)
- *The Outsiders* (from S.E. Hinton)
- *Pride and Prejudice* (from Jane Austen)
- *The Princess Bride* (from William Goldman)
- *The Secret Garden* (from Frances Hodgson Burnett)
- *Tarzan* (from Edgar Rice Burroughs)
- *The Adventures of Huckleberry Finn* (several versions— from Mark Twain)
- *The Three Musketeers* (from Alexandre Dumas)

> *"Never judge a book by its movie."*
>
> —J. W. Eagan

- *To Kill a Mockingbird* (from Harper Lee)
- *Treasure Island* (from Robert Louis Stevenson)
- *Wuthering Heights* (from Emily Bronte)

- **Listen to audiobooks**, especially when traveling, exercising, biking, hiking, etc. as substitutes for listening to music on iPods, watching DVDs or playing electronic games. Research is showing that listening is just as effective as reading with the eyes. You'll find more resources and information in the **"Recommended Resources"** section at the back of this book.

- **Join (or start) a book club.** Join a book club together in your area, or start one of your own. Explore individual book clubs, as well as parent/child ones. Your local librarian or bookseller can help.

- **Start a collection.** Charms, buttons, postcards, coins, baseball cards, stamps, autographs . . . becoming a discerning collector might just motivate your son or daughter to read up on the subject, and you'll have a built-in gift, giving opportunity to boot. How about collecting *books*—by author, genre, subject, style—or signed books, first editions, biographies, etc.?

- **Experiment with "armchair travel."** Take advantage of an upcoming (or recent) family trip, or that of another family member or friend, to explore travel-related fiction and nonfiction.

- **Make a time capsule.** This is a great way for kids to express their feelings and thoughts about their lives and their world to future generations. A time capsule need not be an elaborate metal cylinder embedded in the cornerstone of a building—it can be as simple as a shoebox full of carefully selected and archived items, reserved for opening until a later date. See page 71 for specific instructions and ideas.

In addition . . .

Promote journalistic activities. Sometimes, seeing their own words and ideas in print can be a huge motivation for young people to write—and read—more. If your child has an area of interest or expertise, or is passionate about a local cause, try getting him or her involved in writing for a local newspaper, a teen magazine, or an "e-zine." Suggest letters to the editor, junior editorials, and even articles on a given subject. There are a number of online resources in this regard—article clearing houses which submit articles free of charge to anyone looking for content for their publications. Two to explore are www.ezinearticles.com and www.goarticles.com.

Recommend posting book reviews online. There are a number of online sites that will post reader reviews, including those written by kids. Among them:

> www.amazon.com
>
> www.bn.com (Barnes & Noble)
>
> www.borders.com
>
> www.kidsbookshelf.com
>
> www.bookhooks.com

Encourage altruism. If your child babysits or does mother's helper activities, suggest a book series that he or she can share with a young charge, one that might hook both of them. You might also look into a youth mentoring program that will provide opportunities to help a younger child learn to read or to develop reading skills. To find one in your area, visit www.mentoring.org, or conduct an Internet search (using Google® or any other search engine provider) on "youth mentoring programs."

What to Read

Continue to supply the following:

- ✎ **Books that fuel passions and interests.** Whose posters are on your child's walls? Whether it's sports, music, fashion, or any other subject of special interest to your child, providing books that speak to a personal passion builds on the association of reading with pleasure. It is also a powerful way to affirm your child's individuality. I mentioned earlier that when our son Sam was very young, he was passionate about trucks. These days, he reads books about baseball (especially the Yankees), *Star Wars* and classic rock, in addition to good fantasy and fiction that sparks his imagination. As long as he's reading for pleasure, we're thrilled.

- **Poetry**—explore anthologies, as well as collections by one particular author.

- **Reference books**—such as dictionaries, encyclopedias, and other reference materials. Ideally, each individual should have his or her own up-to-date, quality dictionary and thesaurus, but even a good family one is fine as long as it is readily available and easy to access. The Internet has just about made bound encyclopedias obsolete, of course, but I still believe in the power and pleasure of thumbing through a physical book for in-depth information.

- **Magazines**—There are many wonderful magazines geared especially toward pre-teens and teens these days. Some examples are:

> *"Magazines all too frequently lead to books and should be regarded by the prudent as the heavy petting of literature."*
>
> —Fran Lebowitz

9–14 years

American Girl (8 to 12 years)

Calliope

Creative Kids

Cricket

Dig

Muse

National Geographic Kids

Sports Illustrated Kids

Time for Kids

But middle schoolers are also ready for "grown-up" magazines that speak to an area of interest—cooking, riding, sailing, etc.

- **Science books**—Fiction, science-fiction, and nonfiction.

- **"Series" books.** Reluctant readers can often be hooked by a book "series" that takes familiar characters on new adventures. Some popular examples for middle school students are:
  - *The Inheritance Series* (Christopher Paolini)
  - *Harry Potter* (J.K. Rowling)
  - *A Series of Unfortunate Events* (Lemony Snicket)
  - *His Dark Materials* (Philip Pullman)

- *The Chronicles of Narnia* (C.S. Lewis)
- *Warriors* (Erin Hunter)
- *Anne of Green Gables* (L.M. Montgomery)
- *Little House on the Prairie* (Laura Ingalls Wilder)
- *Septimus Heap* (Angie Sage)
- *The Wednesday Tales* (Jon Berkeley)
- *The Dark is Rising* (Susan Cooper)
- *The Chronicles of Prydain* (Lloyd Alexander)
- *Artemis Fowl* (Eoin Colfer)
- *Redwall* (Brian Jacques)

- **"How-To" Books.** "How-To's" can often make for engaging reading when time does not allow for getting involved in a whole story—in the bathroom, for instance.

- **Comic books and graphic novels.** For reluctant readers, or those with reading challenges, these can provide a portal to discovering the pleasure of books. Nonfiction and classics are now also available in graphic book form. See the related entry in the previous chapter for details.

In addition, offer . . .

Books about characters handling middle-school emotions and experiences—school and social issues, peer pressure, moving, relationships. Middle schoolers can have a broad range of reading skills, but they are generally ready for chapter books and novels, especially when read aloud.

Riddle and joke books. Keep them laughing—and delighting their friends—with an assortment of good joke, riddle, and trivia books. (In our house, these tend to be especially appreciated in the bathroom, when lighter reading is sometimes called for.)

Books on puberty and adolescent issues. Important caveat: This has to be done *artfully!* The pre-teen and teenage years are ripe with self-consciousness and hormone-driven feelings, questions, and concerns. While your child may not feel comfortable openly discussing it all with you, *tactfully* providing books that de-mystify puberty and emerging sexuality can be a true and timely gift. Some families find it helpful to leave the book strategically placed in a spot where a child can "happen" upon it and read it privately at his or her leisure.

Books written by peers. Even the most reluctant reader is often intrigued by the notion of a book that was written by a peer . . . especially if it was later turned into a movie. Many even become inspired to try their hand at writing a book themselves. Here are a few to look into:

> *"A book is like a garden, carried in the pocket."*
>
> —Chinese proverb

- ✆ *Eragon—The Inheritance Series* (Christopher Paolini)
- ✆ *The Outsiders* (S.E. Hinton)
- ✆ *This Can't Be Happening at McDonald Hall* (Gordon Korman)

Historical fiction—If your child is intrigued by a particular period of history—the Middle Ages, for instance, or the Civil War—historical fiction may well appeal. Set against the backdrop of a particular period in history, these books feature famous characters from history in imagined or enlarged upon situations, or fictional characters in historic places or circumstances.

Biographies and autobiographies—Biographies can be great reading for a young person who is passionate about a particular figure, era, issue, or subject.

Survival stories, in which characters battle nature or adversity. (Caveat: Know your child . . . I would always strive to choose those that provide hope or triumph in the long run.)

Motivational books. Some kids simply don't enjoy fiction, or books about "teens in peril," etc. In this case, an inspirational series like *Chicken Soup for the Teenage Soul* (Jack Canfield/Mark Victor Hansen/Kimberly Kirberger/Mitch Claspy) can sometimes be just the ticket.

The "classics." There's a reason they're considered classic! Depending on your child, middle school can be the ideal time to introduce the *great* books, such as those by Charles Dickens, Mark Twain, Jane Austen, the Bronte sisters, Alexandre Dumas, etc., especially as family read-alouds.

Reading Techniques

As always, the most important principles to keep in mind when reading with young people—including teenagers—are:

1. **Invite participation.** Engage your listeners in the story by stopping occasionally to ask a question, draw a parallel with their own lives, point something out, invite a prediction, etc.

2. **Enlist other family members, friends, and *teachers* in the read-aloud process.** Just as vital as continuing to read aloud with older kids is involving others in that process. It's particularly important to have men—dads, granddads, uncles, etc.—as reading rolemodels (especially for boys).

Also, encourage your child's teachers to continue reading aloud to the class. This can be tricky to achieve, but has *huge* value for older students. If you have any lingering doubts, read the ultra-short chapters 43–48 of Daniel Pennac's *Better Than Life*, which describes the extraordinary gift of a high school teacher who re-awakened his students' love of books by reading aloud to them. Here's a sample:

> *"The pleasure of reading was close at hand, held hostage in these adolescents by a secret and very old fear: the fear of not understanding.*
>
> *They had forgotten what a book was, and what it had to offer. They had forgotten that, above all else, a novel <u>tells a story</u>. They didn't realize that a novel must be read as a novel. And that its first job is to quench our thirst for stories.*
>
> *To fulfill that need, they turned to the small screen. It did its assembly-line job, grinding out cartoons, series, soap operas, and thrillers in a string of interchangeable stereotypes. That was their ration of fiction. It filled their heads the way fast food fills the stomach. It stuffed them, but it didn't stick to the ribs. Digestion was immediate. But they were hungry again right after the meal."*

The following tips have been separated into three groups: **Developing Listening/Critical Thinking Skills; Read-Aloud Skills;** and **Maximizing Interest.** And remember, if your middle schooler is reluctant to be read to, or feels it's "babyish," visit the "Special Situations and Frequently Asked Questions" section of this book for more specific engagement strategies.

Developing Listening/Critical Thinking Skills

Continue to . . .

- ✎ **Relate books to others you have read in the past.** Draw parallels and make distinctions between plotlines, issues, writing styles, or character choices.
- ✎ **Follow up on stories.** Look for opportunities to make connections or draw parallels between what you are reading together and real life. *"This reminds me of that scene in the book when..."* provides an opening for further dialogue and creates important connections between reading and everyday life.

Read-Aloud Skills

As outlined in the previous chapters...

- ✎ **Set the stage before you begin.** If you're picking up where you left off from a previous reading experience, begin by discussing what you read yesterday and what might happen next. If it's a new book, begin by introducing the title, author, and illustrator, and by studying the cover together.
- ✎ **Slow down.** Don't read so slowly as to be labored or dull, but do pause for emphasis here and there, and take your time to "spin" the tale.
- ✎ **Maintain color in your voice.** Avoid monotones...try to enliven the experience for your listeners by employing a whisper here, emphasis there.
- ✎ **End sentences with periods instead of question marks.** Avoid upward inflections at the end of sentences, or *leaning* into the next sentence before the last has been fully absorbed. Allow each "thought" to exist by itself before moving on to the next. (Re-read page 47 for details on this technique.)

Maximizing Interest

Continue to . . .

- ✎ **Use character voices or accents** to bring the individual characters in the story to life.
- ✎ **Stop reading at a suspenseful point in a book.** Try to leave your listeners wanting more, and looking forward to the next installment.

Emma's Family Favorites for Middle School and Beyond

"The question we need to ask of a story is this: does it illuminate what is true in significant ways? A good book is not problem centered; it is people centered. It reveals how to be a human being and what the possibilities of life are; it offers hope."

—**Gladys Hunt,** *Honey for a Child's Heart*

The definition of middle school varies from state to state and from school to school—some begin as early as 5th grade, others consider it to be 6th–8th, or just 7th and 8th. In terms of reading recommendations, much depends on your individual child and the level at which he or she is reading.

Many of the books recommended for elementary school students—especially the chapter books and novels—remain appropriate during middle school. Children react to books differently depending on their age, and can truly enjoy revisiting an old favorite with the fresh perspective that a few years can provide. Books that were initially enjoyed for story and plot later become intriguing because of character development or identification, and still later for their themes, allegories, and literary devices.

Here are some of our additional family favorites for the middle school years and beyond:

The Adventures of Tom Sawyer (Mark Twain)
The classic novel celebrating all that boyhood embraces—adventure (and some mischief) mixed with life lessons and humor along the way. Girls and boys alike will cherish and remember this gem.

> **The Adventures of Huckleberry Finn**—*The sequel to Tom Sawyer, also a masterpiece. While it delves into somewhat weightier issues (religion, racism), its portrait of rural life and sympathetic hero is riveting to young readers.*

Anne Frank: The Diary of a Young Girl (Anne Frank)
The classic journal recording a young girl's family struggles during two years of hiding from the Nazis in war-torn Holland.

Anne of Green Gables series (Lucy Maud Montgomery)
One of the most enjoyable series in children's literature, chronicling the antics of Anne Shirley, a red-headed orphan girl, adopted by a pair of farmers on Prince Edward Island during the early part of the 20th century.

Around the World in Eighty Days (Jules Verne)
The classic favorite, in which Phileas Fogg and his manservant set out to win a bet by traveling around the world in eighty days.

The Black Stallion (Walter Farley)
A powerful story about a boy and his horse that makes a lifetime impression on readers, whether equestrians or not.

Blue Wolf (Catherine Creedon)
Fourteen-year old Jamie spends the summer with his mysterious aunt in the wilds of the Pacific Northwest, and discovers some long-hidden family secrets—including the ability to shape-shift to wolf form.

Chasing Vermeer (Blue Balliett/Brett Helquist)
Two sixth-graders attempt to solve the crime of a stolen Vermeer painting. Fun illustrations offer puzzles in and of themselves.

The City of Ember (**Books of Ember series**) (Jeanne DuPrau)
In a post-apocalyptic society, two twelve-year-olds set out on a mission to find the light.

The Chronicles of Narnia (C.S. Lewis)
Four children visit an enchanted world where they transcend being "just children." Timeless themes of good and evil, eloquently told, and brimming with adventure and wonderful characters.

The Chronicles of Prydain (Lloyd Alexander)
Humor, honor, courage, fantasy, a hero's journey—along with assistant pig keepers, frustrated ex-giants, witches, and all manner of other wonderfully eccentric characters, make this series based on the Welsh legend a must.

Crispin, Cross of Lead (Avi)
The prolific Avi tackles the Middle Ages in this ripping-good yarn about a boy accused of a crime he didn't commit, who discovers his true identity in the process.

> **The True Confessions of Charlotte Doyle**—*an 1832 teenager's adventures on a sailing vessel crossing the Atlantic.*

Fever 1793 (Laurie Halse Anderson)
Compelling historical fiction about a willful sixteen-year-old girl's coming of age during the Yellow Fever epidemic of Philadelphia in 1793.

Freaky Friday (Mary Rodgers)
A mother and daughter switch bodies for a day and gain a new appreciation for what it's like to be the other, as well as for being themselves.

The Golden Compass (Philip Pullman)
The first in Pullman's epic trilogy, **His Dark Materials**, *about a young girl's quest for truth in a parallel universe in which people have daemons; witches, gypsies and armored bears abound; and "dust" has the power to control destiny and unite worlds. The other titles in this unforgettable series are:*

> **The Subtle Knife**

> **The Amber Spyglass**

Harry Potter and the Sorcerer's Stone (J.K. Rowling)
The first in the staggeringly successful series about a young boy's adventures at wizard school that revolutionized the middle-grade reading world.

Hotheads (Gen LeRoy)
Twelve-year-old Geneva copes with troubles at school and at home, but remains an indomitable spirit.

> **Cold Feet**—*The sequel to Hotheads, Geneva tries to take charge of her life by dressing as a boy and gets involved in a gambling ring.*

The Invention of Hugo Cabret (Brian Selznick)
An innovative book that blends text and artwork to spin the tale of an orphan boy who lives in, and tends the clocks for, a Paris train station. Though substantial in size, Selznick uses many pages of illustration to further the story before picking up with the text once again.

A Long Way from Chicago (Richard Peck)
*Joey and Mary Alice spend a week "downstate" with Grandma Dowdel every summer—and are continuously astounded by her outlandish behavior and hilarious antics, in this series of stories satirizing small-town life. The equally delightful sequel is **A Year Down Yonder**.*

The Little Grey Men (B.B.)
The last three gnomes in Britain set off down-stream to find their missing brother. Brimming with the joys of nature and adventure.

The Little House on the Prairie series (Laura Ingalls Wilder)
The classic series chronicling Laura Ingalls Wilder's youth on the prairie during pioneer times.

The Midwife's Apprentice (Karen Cushman)
A coming-of-age tale set during the Middle Ages about a feisty, homeless orphan girl who apprentices with the local midwife.

My Family and Other Animals (Gerald Durrell)
The delightful account of Durrell's childhood growing up on the Greek island of Corfu with his eccentric English family and a host of visitors, both human and animal.

> **The Battle for Castle Cockatrice**—*Three children and some eccentric talking animals attempt to restore peace to the land of Mythologia.*

My Side of the Mountain (Jean Craighead George)
When young Sam runs away to the Catskills and takes up residence in a hollowed tree, he learns a lot about living off the land—and even more about growing up.

> **Julie of the Wolves**—*A young orphan with Eskimo roots runs away and finds her new family amongst the wolves of the Alaskan tundra.*

The 101 Dalmatians (Dodie Smith)
The delightful original book that inspired the classic Disney film, in which two Dalmatians set out to rescue their puppies from the wicked Cruella DeVille.

> ### The Starlight Barking
> *The surprisingly good and gently philosophical sequel to **The 101 Dalmatians**, in which the Dalmatian family—and all dogs in England—awaken one day to find everyone on earth but dogs asleep.*

***The Palace of Laughter* ("The Wednesday Tales" series)** (Jon Berkeley)
The first in a hilarious trilogy chronicling the adventures of orphan Miles Wednesday, his friend Little—a fallen song angel—and an eccentric circus. The further adventures are:

> ### The Tiger's Egg
> ### The Lightning Key

***The Penderwicks* series** (Jeanne Birdsall)
Four sisters, their absent-minded widower father, a dog—and a good deal of hilarious hijinks.

The Phantom Tollbooth (Norton Juster)
The classic tale of Milo, a bored child who drives his toy car through a toy tollbooth and ends up in a magical world of letters and numbers.

The Pushcart War (Jean Merrill)
New York City pushcart peddlers take on big business and corrupt government when they go to "war" with the big trucks that clog the streets of the city. A funny and shrewd satire that, though written over fifty years ago, remains powerfully resonant.

Roll of Thunder, Hear My Cry (Mildred D. Taylor)
The bittersweet and deeply moving story of the Logan family and their fight against racial injustice, poverty, and betrayal in Depression-era Mississippi.

Saffy's Angel (Hilary McKay)
A young girl growing up in an eccentric English family learns she is actually an adopted cousin, and sets out in search of a stone angel that may contain answers to her questions. The first in a lively series about the Casson family.

A Single Shard (Linda Sue Park)
The Newbery Award–winning tale of a 12th-century Korean orphan who finds himself through his interest in pottery. The book gracefully tackles timeless issues, like the nature of home, and art, and the ownership of creative ideas.

The Sword in the Stone (T.H. White)
The extraordinary tale of young Prince Arthur, his tutor Merlin, the wise magician, and the adventures leading up to Arthur's legendary extraction of the sword from the stone.

To Kill a Mockingbird (Harper Lee)
The heart-wrenching, Pulitzer Prize–winning story of a young girl coming of age in the deep south, and her lawyer father, who risks everything to defend a black man accused of a crime he didn't commit.

The Twenty-One Balloons (William Pene DuBois)
A professor intending to fly across the ocean lands on Krakatoa and encounters a host of eccentric wonders.

Watership Down (Richard Adams)
An extraordinary, allegorical novel about freedom, ethics, and human nature—told from the perspective of wild rabbits. Written for adults, but equally enjoyed and appreciated by older kids.

The Wind in the Willows (Kenneth Grahame)
The classic adventure story, set in early 20th-century Britain, featuring the lovable characters Rat, Toad, Mole, and Badger. A must.

The Wish (Gail Carson Levine)
An eighth grader is granted one wish—to be the most popular girl at her school—and ultimately learns the meaning and value of true friendship.

> **Ella Enchanted**—*A delightfully fresh, imaginative, and award-winning take on Cinderella.*

The Wolves of Willoughby Chase (Joan Aiken)
Two Victorian girls, a wicked governess, wolves, a cruel orphanage, adventure, and romance make this, the first book in Aiken's wonderful series of Gothic thrillers, **The Wolves Chronicles**, *a delicious read.*

A Wrinkle in Time series (Madeleine L'Engle)
A coming-of-age fantasy in which Meg, her younger brother, and her friend travel through time and space searching for Meg's father, a scientist who disappeared while researching a "wrinkle in time."

6

Special Situations and Frequently Asked Questions

"A book, too, can be a star ... a living fire to lighten the darkness, leading out into the expanding universe."

—Madeleine L'Engle, author

"What about children with special needs—Dyslexia, ADD, learning disabilities, on the autism spectrum, or who have other challenges? Do these techniques apply to them?"

This is a huge subject, worthy of filling the pages of many books alone, and, of course, every situation has its own unique set of issues and attendant recommendations. The good news is that reading can be enjoyed, and comprehension skills and strategies can be learned, even by individuals with extreme learning disabilities. The key lies in a multilayered approach that incorporates teachers, therapists, and parents.

The challenge is that children with learning disabilities may find the struggle to read (or simply to concentrate) enormously frustrating—and the associated feelings of failure that may arise can be devastating. For this reason, the philosophy and strategies set forth in this book may be even *more* important. Actions like reading with your child, supporting and promoting literacy through everyday activities, and being a good role model as a reader are gifts that you, as a parent, are uniquely equipped to provide.

Specific suggestions for using this approach for children with special needs include the following:

- **An even greater emphasis on read-aloud.** Most children's listening skills are stronger than their reading skills, and they can therefore comprehend more if they read along silently as you read the book out aloud. Audiobooks with accompanying texts are another great way to pair reading and listening. When working with read-aloud, begin with short passages, and extend the time if your child maintains focus.

- Even though the English language is complex, dyslexic children *can* learn phonics—but they need **a sequential, multi-sensory, structured reading program** and solid reading support at home. This includes reading together, playing games that isolate sounds or build words, and many of the other activities and recommendations in this book. According to the International Dyslexia Association (www.interdys.org), "If children who are dyslexic get effective phonological training in Kindergarten and 1st grade, they will have significantly fewer problems in learning to read at grade level than do children who are not identified or helped until 3rd grade. But it is never too late for individuals with dyslexia to learn to read, process and express information more efficiently. Research shows that programs utilizing multi-sensory structured language techniques can help children and adults learn to read."

- Encourage your child to **look and listen for the five W's**: *Who* are the main characters, *where* and *when* does the story take place, *what* conflicts do the characters face, and *why* do they act as they do? For a child with learning disabilities, this can greatly aid comprehension.

- **Become your child's advocate.** Don't worry about being a nag or asking too many questions at school. You have a right to receive answers when it comes to your child, and he or she may be eligible to receive extra support and accommodations that you may not even be aware of. Don't assume that the "experts"—teachers, administrators, doctors, and the like— will always come forward with information or recommendations specific to your child. Ask, and ask again.

✎ Above all, **do your own homework.** The greatest gift we can give our children is to learn all we can about who they are as individuals and what their unique needs and issues are. There are many different types of programs and resources, even within the multi-sensory or phonics-based approaches—and many different opinions as to best practices with respect to learning challenges. With the wealth of information now available via the Internet, there is no reason to be in the dark about your child's special needs. Research everything you can, and get first, second, and third opinions. In this way, you can make informed choices that are specific to your individual child. As the parent, *you* are the only one who has the entire picture, and your child's future success depends on your active involvement and advocacy.

Additional information and support can be found through a wide number of resources, most notably:

✎ **Reading Rockets**—A national multimedia project offering information and resources on how young kids learn to read, why so many struggle, and how caring adults can help. www.readingrockets.org

✎ **Learning Disabilities Association of America**—National and local support for, and cutting edge information on, learning disabilities, with practical solutions and a comprehensive network of resources. www.ldanatl.org

✎ **LD Online**—Information and advice about learning disabilities and ADHD. www.ldonline.org

✎ **Internet Special Education Resources**—A nationwide directory of professionals, organizations, and schools that serve the learning disabilities and special education communities. www.iser.com

✎ **International Dyslexia Association**—www.interdys.org

✎ **Reading from Scratch**—Program for dyslexia. www.dyslexia.org

✎ **Center for Learning Differences**—Resources for families and professionals dealing with learning issues. www.centerforlearningdifferences.org

✎ **Bookshare.org**—Provides print-disabled people in the United States with access to over 37,100 books and 150 periodicals that are converted to Braille, large print, or digital formats for text to speech audio. www.bookshare.org

- ↪ **_Launching Young Readers_**—A series of half-hour PBS television programs that look at different reading strategies to help young children learn to read, with practical advice for parents. Available as a boxed VHS set or as a DVD with bonus material. A viewer guide and a family guide are included. http://www.learningstore.org/we1018vk.html
- ↪ **Reading Window**—Methods for preventing and reversing reading problems. www.readingwindow.org

"At what age should a child learn to read or be able to read?"

Children usually begin to sound out words or recognize them by sight somewhere between four and seven years of age. Needless to say, this process is greatly facilitated if the child has been exposed to books and other printed materials from an early age. Learning to read fluently and with comprehension by the end of 3rd grade traditionally marks the difference between the "learning to read" phase of development and "reading to learn." By the time they enter 4th grade, students are expected to have developed the basic ability to recognize words on the basis of their spelling or sequence.

"When I look back, I am so impressed again by the life giving power of literature. If I were a young person today, trying to gain a sense of myself in the world, I would do that again by reading, just as I did when I was young."

—Maya Angelou

Having said that, it's vitally important that we allow reading to unfold for each child in its own time and at its own pace. It's interesting to note, for instance, that Finland ranks among the highest reading scores in the world, despite the fact that formal reading is not taught in Finnish schools until seven years of age.

It's also important to remember that most children can understand and absorb a book that is *read to them* at a much higher level than they can read themselves. For this reason, it is important not to "read down" to kids, but rather to invite them to "stretch up" when reading aloud. (Assuming, of course, that the material is appropriate for them, socially and emotionally speaking.)

"I keep hearing the words 'fluency' and 'comprehension' relative to my child's reading. Can you help me understand these issues better?"

"Fluency" is defined as the ability to read text with speed, accuracy, and proper expression. Fluent readers recognize words automatically, read aloud smoothly and with expression, do not have to concentrate on decoding, and can focus on meaning.

Problems in fluency occur when a child can pronounce words but reads or decodes so slowly that meaning and expression are lost. There are a number of activities that can greatly enhance fluency, including:

- **Modeled Reading:** In which a child listens to someone else modeling fluent reading—a parent, teacher, caregiver, or reading buddy—in read-aloud format, or on audiobooks.

- **Guided Reading:** When a child receives assistance from an adult, older child, or peer, through activities like:
  - **Choral Reading**—reading aloud alongside other children or adults.
  - **Peer/Paired Reading**—children, or a child and adult, take turns reading.
  - **Echo Reading**—the child "echoes" what he/she has heard by reading it back.
  - **Tape Assisted Reading**—listening to and reading along with a tape or audiobook.
  - **Buddy Reading**—an older child listens to, reads with, and offers feedback to a younger child.

- **Practice and Performance:** Children develop prosody (proper phrasing and expression) through activities like:
  - **Repeated Reading**—reading the same text over again until fluency is achieved.
  - **Independent Reading**—reading silently to oneself, and periodically checking in with a listener.
  - **Reader's Theater**—rehearsed oral performances of scripts adapted from children's books.
  - **Oral Recitation**—selected passages are read loud and/or acted out.

Reading "comprehension" refers to the level of understanding of a passage or text, and is generally measured by a student's ability to summarize or answer questions about what he or she has read. There is considerable debate in the education world as to whether children need to learn to analyze and comprehend text even *before* they can read it on their own, or whether they must first learn how to decode the words through phonics before they can analyze the story itself.

As with fluency, proficient reading comprehension depends on the ability to recognize words quickly and effortlessly. If students must use too much of their processing capacity to read individual words, this can interfere with their ability to comprehend what is read. Strategies to enhance comprehension include building vocabulary, and asking for predictions, summaries, and answers to questions about a given text.

While parents can certainly employ some or all of these techniques at home to support their child's reading, it's always best to do in consultation and partnership with a trusted teacher. If the child begins to feel *too* much pressure, or the emphasis shifts from the joy of reading to reading achievement, there's a good chance they will develop a negative association or get turned off altogether. As always, the prime focus should be on building those connections between reading and pleasure, and minimizing those that suggest chore, pressure, or obligation.

"My child seems to be really struggling in learning to read. How can I help, and how do I know if he has a problem?"

According to Reading Rockets (www.readingrockets.org),

> "Learning to read is a challenge for almost 40 percent of kids. The good news is that with early help, most reading problems can be prevented. The bad news is that 44 percent of parents who notice their child having trouble wait a year or more before getting help. Unfortunately, the older a child is, the more difficult it is to teach him or her to read. The window of opportunity closes early for most kids. If a child can't read well by the end of third grade, odds are that he or she will never catch up. And the effects of falling behind and feeling like a failure can be devastating."

Not all children learn to read at the same time, of course, but there are certain milestones that can help you gauge how well your child is doing compared with others his or her age. The main thing is, *if you suspect a difficulty, don't hesitate to take action.* Although it's never too late to help a child, reading problems are best addressed when caught at a young age.

Talk to your child's teacher and consider having your child tested for hearing problems, learning disabilities, or any number of other issues that might be affecting his or her abilities. Even if your child attends a private or parochial school, you can request that your local public school do an assessment (for which there is no charge), or you can hire a licensed professional in private practice to do so.

A thorough psycho-educational assessment will help determine the exact nature of a child's reading difficulties. It should clarify whether the primary reading problem is poor fluency, with comprehension problems a secondary issue, or whether there are other problems that contribute to comprehension, such as vision or hearing issues. Some children end up being diagnosed with a learning disability, but there is an even larger group who never receive a diagnosis but who nonetheless need targeted assistance to learn and read well.

> "Drill and skill don't motivate. What motivates children and adults to read is (1) they like the experience a lot, (2) they like the subject matter a lot, and (3) they like and follow the lead of people who read a lot."
>
> —Jim Trelease, *The Read-Aloud Handbook*

Once the exact nature of the problem has been identified, you can work with your child's teacher or assessor to determine which of the many different reading support programs available is best for your child. A good reading program addresses the specific needs of each individual child, balances fun and creativity with learning, and presents information in a way that is most beneficial to the child's own unique learning style. There is no one perfect method for teaching reading, and no one method works for everyone.

The most important thing is that parents, teachers, and other professionals begin talking and strategizing how they can work *together* to help an individual child overcome or cope with his or her reading difficulties. It takes everyone working as a unified team to help a child strengthen the skills that are so crucial to learning to read.

Having said all that, I do want to make a final but important point. It's not unusual for parents to become nearly obsessive in their efforts to manage their child's learning and development. Learning to read is hard, and can be challenging even for children with no learning issues whatsoever. It takes time and practice to develop the understanding, vocabulary, fluency, and comprehension skills necessary to make reading easy and pleasurable. If your child senses you hovering too much, or feels unduly pressured by your expectations or micromanagement, this can actually run counter to your best intentions. Try to balance your ambitions for your child with plenty of patience and support, and remember that the key lies first and foremost in seeking ways to underscore the connection between reading and joy.

"How do we educate the heart? There are really only two ways: life experience and stories about life experience, which is called literature. All the great preachers and all the great teachers of the heart have used stories to get their lesson plan across – Aesop, Socrates, Confucius, Moses, and Jesus – stories about mustard seeds and shepherds and vineyards and prostitutes and fishermen and travelers. It is the power of story to educate upstairs as well as downstairs."

—Jim Trelease,
The Read-Aloud Handbook

Some additional resources:

Early Intervention Services—Most states provide an Early Intervention Program (EIP) as part of the national Early Intervention Program for infants and toddlers with disabilities and their families. First created by Congress in 1986 under the Individuals with Disabilities Education Act (IDEA), the EIP is usually administered by the State Department of Health through the Bureau of Early Intervention.

http://www.readingsuccesslab.com—assessment and intervention products for home and school settings

http://www.pta.org—National Parent/Teacher Association

http://www.nectac.org—National Early Childhood Technical Assistance Center

"My son doesn't want me to read to him anymore. He thinks it's babyish. What can I do?"

The wonderful author and self-proclaimed "certified readiologist" Esmé Raji Codell (www.planetesme.com) offers some wonderful strategies for enticing older kids who feel they've outgrown being read to, which I'll paraphrase here:

Be honest. Explain to your child that you know he is a great reader—this is simply very important to *you*. Say that reading aloud is a family tradition, part of who you are as a parent and something you love to do, a gift you are trying to give. Ask for his trust in you. Add that it is something you hope he will grow up to do with his own kids.

Wheedle a little. *"Did I not do things for you all day? So now do this one thing for me."* Okay, a guilt trip—but it may work, and once you start, they'll be begging for more.

Go to bed later. Let your kids stay up half an hour later if they'll listen to you read.

Try it for a week. Tell them that if they still don't like it at the end of the trial period, you'll stop. Then serialize a novel, and they'll be hooked.

Be flexible about timing. Bedtime may not always work—but how about during breakfast? Dinner? Before homework? While they wash dishes? On Sundays? Just pick one time that *does* work, and make it consistent.

Try guest readers. The other parent, a grandparent, a friend, an older sibling. Even an audiobook—but one you listen to together and can follow along with the real book.

Take turns. You read a page, your child reads a page—or a chapter.

Let them choose. Tell them they can pick what they want you to read, as long as you can read it aloud. If you don't trust their judgment, tell them they get one pick and you get one pick.

Give in, but read alongside. Fighting about it is counterproductive. If your child is still really resistant, you can still model read-aloud with your spouse or partner. You can get book lights and read silently alongside your child. You can have a quiet family reading time—everyone together in the same room, by the fire, reading independently.

"My kids are in high school. Is it too late to help them develop a love of reading?"

Maybe not. It's all about finding the right hook—and the right book. You might try some of these techniques:

Older children will be more likely to read something recommended by a friend or peer rather than an adult. If your child has a friend who enjoys reading, try asking that friend to make a recommendation to your child.

Enlist your child's teacher and librarian. You might be able to request that he or she assign or read a particular book to the class that you know your child—and his or her peers—would enjoy. You also might be able to enlist their aid in a "stealth" plan to get your child hooked on reading. If they don't believe in reading to their students, give them a copy of Daniel Pennac's *Better Than Life* for inspiration.

Provide books on your child's heroes and passions. Whose posters are on your kid's bedroom walls? Be they sports figures, musicians, movie or TV stars, poets, scientists, or other classic or contemporary heroes, chances are someone has written a book about them. There may also be fictional stories that deal with a subject your child is passionate about, or that are set in a world they love, such as horseback riding, baseball, or the fashion or music industry. I have a fashion-conscious teenage friend who found her passion for reading through the *Gossip Girl* series (Cecily von Ziegesar). Find the right book, and they might just get hooked.

Try nonfiction. When parents think of books for teens, they usually think of novels—fantasy, sci-fi, schoolyard drama, or zany antics. Teachers tend to mostly assign fictional stories, poems, or plays as required reading, and expect free-reading selections to be fictional as well. But if you have a reluctant reader on your hands, you might just find that nonfiction does the trick. Some teens prefer biographies of real-life people to a made-up, teen-in-trouble story, or books on real science rather than science fiction. Some respond better to motivational or inspirational books—like the *Chicken Soup* series, for instance. The most important thing is to find something your child will agree to read . . . and will *enjoy* reading.

Try a little "bibliotherapy." If you know your child is dealing with some particular problem or issue at school, leave a carefully selected book—fiction or nonfiction—that deals with that topic on his or her bed or desk.

Bring home an assortment of magazines and library books, and leave them lying around. A bored teen might pick one up.

Engage their altruism. If your child babysits, suggest a book series that he or she can share with a young charge, one that might hook both of them. You might also look into a youth mentoring program that your child can participate in, one that will provide opportunities for him or her to help a younger child learn to read or develop his or her reading skills. To find one in your area, visit www.mentoring.org, or conduct an Internet search (using Google or any other search engine provider) on "youth mentoring programs."

Allow comic books and graphic novels. For reluctant readers, or those with reading challenges, these can often provide a portal to discovering the pleasure of books. See the detailed entries on graphic novels in the Middle School and Elementary School sections for recommendations and further resources.

> "The more you read, the better you get at it; the better you get at it, the more you like it; and the more you like it, the more you do it."
>
> —Jim Trelease,
> *The Read-Aloud Handbook*

Try books or articles written by kids. Even the most reluctant reader is often intrigued by the notion of something that was written by a peer . . . especially if it's published or was later turned into a movie. Many even become inspired to try their hand at writing something themselves.

Promote journalistic activities. Try getting your child involved in writing for a local newspaper, a teen magazine, or an "e-zine." Suggest a letter to the editor, a junior editorial, or even an article about a local cause or personal passion. Sometimes seeing their own words and ideas in print can be a huge motivation for young people to write— and read—more. There are also a number of online resources in this regard—one to check out is Teen Ink, (http://www.teenink.com). There are also article clearing houses, which submit articles free of charge to anyone looking for content for their publications. Two to explore are www.ezinearticles.com and www.goarticles.com.

If all else fails . . . barter, bribe, or bargain. Try a little incentive-based reading. Just make sure that the choice of reading material is *really* sensational, and will appeal to your individual child—you want to make the most of this opportunity, and maximize the chances of your child getting hooked.

"Isn't it the job of schools and teachers to get kids reading?"

Your child may learn to read and write at school—and he or she may even grow to be proficient at it. But research shows that by far the greatest influences on a child's reading abilities and interest are those at home. Teachers may teach your child *how* to read; you will be the one to teach your child to *love* reading. Again, it's all about creating those associations with pleasure and empowerment. Reading that is associated with assessment, grading, testing, pressure, topics of varying interest, "drill and skill," and the like—which is often the bulk of what reading at school ends up being—is more likely to turn kids *away* from reading than entice them toward it. Studies show that children who are read to daily at home, live in an environment with ample access to books, and/or frequent the library on a regular basis are over *seventy-five percent* more likely to maintain an interest in reading in later life than those whose only exposure is at school. There are also studies that show that kids need to have *heard* 1,000 hours of reading in order to succeed in school. Those kind of numbers can't be achieved at school alone.

"I don't believe that class time should be taken up with reading, either alone or by the teacher. Kids can do that on their own time—school is for learning!"

First of all, if your child's teacher—or school—provides both independent reading time in class *and* regular read-aloud time with students, *celebrate*!

"Sustained Silent Reading" (or SSR, also sometimes called "Sustained, Quiet, Un-interrupted Reading Time"—SQUIRT, "Daily Individual Reading Time"—DIRT, "Drop Everything and Read"—DEAR, or "Free Voluntary Reading"—FVR) is an opportunity to experience the joy of reading for reading's sake . . . no interruptions, assignments, grades, or pressures. It therefore connects reading with the concept of *recreation*. It enables kids to see their peers and teacher reading (positive role modeling), and for some it may be the *only* opportunity they have for quiet reading time. Finally, it affords quality practice time in an environment that is supportive of individual needs and levels; the teacher helps identify "just-right books" for each student, which greatly enhances comprehension and enjoyment and is critical for achieving fluency. Think of it as the best kind of "reading lab."

Now, with respect to teachers reading aloud. First of all, it's a documented fact that there is no greater advertisement for reading, and all its attendant pleasures and benefits, than the act of read-aloud (or being read to). A

> *"What if, instead of demanding that students read, the teacher decided to share the joy of reading?"*
>
> —Daniel Pennac, *Better Than Life*

teacher who reads aloud to the class is one more positive reading role-model in your child's life, and is greatly increasing your child's chances of becoming a joyful reader by building on the association of reading with pleasure. But there are huge learning benefits as well. Remember that it isn't until around eighth grade that young people's reading abilities and listening skills *converge*—meaning that until that point, children can understand a great deal more of what is read *to* them than they are able to read to themselves, both in terms of vocabulary *and* ideas. This is reason enough to continue reading aloud with kids through middle school.

Finally, consider this statistic: *Decreased interest in reading can be directly correlated to a decrease in read-aloud time.* As kids get older, they are less likely to be read to, both at home and at school, and their own reading time is more likely to be associated with homework and pressure. Here's where the subtle balance shifts, and reading begins to be associated with "chore." In the words of the great "readiologist" Esmé Raji Codell, "Read-aloud has the power not only to sustain but also to *resuscitate* an interest in and affection for the printed word for children of all ages."

Why wouldn't we want that in the classroom as well as at home?

"Between homework, after school activities, sports, music lessons, and the like, my kid literally has *no time* to read!"

I sympathize. I'm the mother of two school-age children, and I juggle two established jobs plus a freelance writing and editing career. I have a marriage to nurture and a home to manage—not to mention life's other little details like bill payments, car maintenance, doctor's appointments, etc. And much as I would love to read before bed, when my head hits that pillow I fall asleep—instantly. Finding time to read is a challenge for many of us.

"Life is a perpetual plot to keep us from reading."

—Daniel Pennac, *Better Than Life*

My experience is, however, that if you want something badly enough, you find a way to make it work. I have carved out a few places in my life where I do manage to read . . . and I consistently look for more. I tend to carry a book in my purse, and read while I'm:

- ✎ In the bathroom
- ✎ On the treadmill at the gym
- ✎ Waiting to pick my son or daughter up from school
- ✎ At the hairdresser
- ✎ On the bus, train, or plane
- ✎ Waiting for an appointment

Assuming your son or daughter has made the connection between reading and pleasure and *wants* to read, you might help by making reading material available to them at times and in places where they are either in transition from one place to the next, waiting for someone or something, or engaged in some activity that reading could accompany—like getting a haircut, or taking a bath, or eating dinner or dessert. (Actually, the latter is an ideal time for family read-aloud. Or, how about reading to them while *they* do dishes?) Suggest trading the earphones for a book once in a while, or install an audiobook on his or her iPod. If motion sickness is not an issue, keep a book in the car, or use travel time to listen to an audiobook. I've found it especially helpful to keep good reading material in all of our bathrooms—and to change it regularly to keep it interesting. You might also try one TV-free night a week, and designate it "reading night." You can read something together as a family, snuggle up in the living room together and read independently, or try one of the other activities that support reading listed in this book, like playing a good board game or engaging in an author/illustrator study.

> *"No matter how busy you may think you are, you must find time for reading, or surrender yourself to self-chosen ignorance."*
>
> — Confucius

"So many of the books out there for older kids nowadays seem dark and depressing, or use language and tackle subjects that run contrary to our value system as parents. I'm afraid of what my kid might be reading!"

I consider myself a ferocious liberal, and I share your concerns. In the introduction to the Middle School section of this book, I talk about my own experiences with my son Sam and the degree to which "depressing" reading assignments were dampening his enthusiasm for reading in general.

My recommendations are twofold: *investigate* and *communicate*.

Stay in touch with what your child is reading, so that you can at the very least have meaningful dialogue with him or her about the themes or issues that are being raised by a given book, and the ideas and language therein. We can't protect our children forever from exposure to the world's darker elements, but we can take the opportunity—while they are still under our roofs—to help them better understand the issues. And by sharing our own value systems with respect to these issues, we can help them to develop their own. The only way to do this meaningfully, however, is to be truly aware of what they are actually reading. Acting on hearsay can be dangerous thing . . . better to read the book yourself, or at the very least, several different reviews of it, and perhaps the sections of the book in question.

The second thing is to communicate directly with your child's teachers, school administrators and librarians. Share your concern and, with absolute respect for them and for the challenges of their jobs, ask for their help. You may find that all it takes is an increased awareness level to better balance the assignments across a given semester. Or you may be able to promote a larger classroom or grade-level dialogue about the issues of concern. If nothing else, this invites healthy discourse and teachable moments. Just be mindful that, in your advocacy, you do not inadvertently embarrass your child—or you may experience the reverse effects of your intentions. Keep it positive.

"Talk to me about TV and the Internet. How can I best use them to my child's advantage?"

Indulge me just a moment while I get on my soapbox.

According to the A.C. Nielsen Company, the average American watches more than *four hours* of television a day. That adds up to 28 hours a week—more than a whole day, and 1,456 hours, the equivalent of sixty days, or two *months*—a year. Take that a step further, and you realize that over an average lifetime of say, seventy-five years, one will have spent *twelve and a half years* staring at the television screen!

Given the percentage of time in a child's week devoted to school, this is time stolen from other activities critical to emotional and physical health, such as outdoor play and exercise, reading, and relating to other human beings.

Now, consider these facts:

- The main business of television is advertising. On average, thirty percent of all programming time is devoted to commercials. It's estimated that the average child sees over 20,000 commercials per year. You can see details and more statistics at http://www.csun.edu/science/health/docs/tv&health.html

- Television overtook newsprint in 1963 as the principal source of information in America. Since that time, the number of severely overweight children in America has more than doubled to 4.7 million, according to the American Academy of Pediatrics (AAP).

- Before finishing elementary school, the average child will have watched 8,000 simulated murders on television, and by age eighteen, the same child will have seen 200,000 televised acts of violence, according to the American Psychiatric Association.

- The majority of television programming in America is now controlled by a handful of large corporations, whose principal goal, like any other business, is to serve the larger agenda of the company that owns them—primarily the support of commercial objectives.

But perhaps one of the most disturbing facts about television is this. Al Gore's groundbreaking book, *The Assault on Reason*, posits that television has become the most powerful force in our lives and has dangerously diminished our capacity for reasoned thinking and open inquiry.

Gore writes about the difference between the quality of "vividness" experienced by television viewers as compared with the "vividness" experienced by readers as follows:

> *"The vividness experienced in the reading of words is automatically modulated by the constant activation of the reasoning centers of the brain. . . . By contrast, the visceral vividness portrayed on television has the capacity to trigger instinctual responses similar to those triggered by reality itself—and without being modulated by logic, reason and reflective thought."*

Gore goes on to explain that, quite literally, we use a different part of our brains when we read versus when we watch television:

> *". . . the parts of the human brain that are central to the reasoning process are continually activated by the very act of reading printed words. . . . Words are composed of abstract symbols—letters—that have no intrinsic meaning themselves until they are strung together into recognizable sequences."*

In fact, the passivity of television watching is actually *"at the <u>expense</u> of activity in parts of the brain associated with abstract thought, logic and the reasoning process."*

Watching television triggers our brain's "orienting response"—our primal instinct to notice sudden movement in our field of vision, and to be "on alert" in case that movement is a predator. The flight-or-fight antennae go up deep in the subconscious. Television—especially commercials and action sequences—repetitively engages those "orienting response" circuits toward fear or arousal on an average of once per second. This has the effect of either numbing our receptors so that it becomes increasingly more difficult to distinguish fantasy from reality (potentially leading to the extreme acts of violence in classrooms and schoolyards that have become a part of our society), or causing a state of hyper-anxiety known as "vicarious traumatization."

Again, to quote Gore,

> *"The physical effects of watching trauma on television—the rise in blood pressure and heart rate—are the same as if an individual has actually experienced the traumatic event directly. Moreover, it has been documented that television can create false memories that are just as powerful as normal memories."*

So, what to do?

We can choose not to own a television of course, or not to allow one in our children's bedrooms. We can moderate the amount of time that we, and they, watch per day or week—all of which are good ideas. But we have to be careful not to create a "forbidden fruit" effect—and one day, when our children are grown, we want them to have the experience and education to make wise choices for themselves and their own children with respect to how they use their leisure time.

"Read as you taste fruit, or savor wine, or enjoy friendship, love or life."

— George Holbrook Jackson

My philosophy is that, as long as they're used *wisely*, both TV and the Internet can complement reading. Young children can read a book about butterflies, and then watch a nature program on TV that shows the magical creatures in vivid color and builds upon the reading experience. They can watch films or shows that have been adapted from books, or that celebrate books and storytelling—such as **Reading Rainbow, Between the Lions, Word World,** or **Sesame Street**.

Older kids can actually learn a great deal about storytelling and dramatic writing from quality television shows. The key, as always, is in your involvement and participation.

Engage kids in dialogue about the scripts of their favorite TV shows. Encourage them to view it as *storytelling*. Point out that someone has written each episode as a story with a beginning, middle, and end, featuring characters in dramatic conflict. Look for any "holes" in the script, when something isn't followed through on or doesn't feel true to character. Or use a TV episode as a point of entry for an important discussion about values, social issues, politics, or the like. Remain aware and involved, and manage television time as you would any other potentially questionable or problematic activity.

The Internet is quite a different animal. Unlike television, it provides broad opportunities for interactivity and exchange. With the important caveat that Internet safety is a separate and unique concern requiring even *greater* parental involvement and supervision, the Internet can be an extraordinary support to literacy in the realms of research, communication, and "the marketplace of ideas." In fact, it may well be the most significant business and communications tool of our era, and computer literacy is now as essential to our children's future as the traditional kind. According to a recent survey conducted by Scholastic,

> *"nearly two thirds of teenagers who are Internet users have extended the reading experience online—from looking for more books by the same author, to visiting websites that immerse a child in content related to a book, to connecting with authors and other readers."*

The Scholastic survey also indicates that after age eight, more children go online daily than read books for fun, and that two thirds of kids age 9–17 believe that within the next ten years, most books that are read for fun will be read digitally, either online or on a handheld computer device. Kids also anticipate that digital books of the future will provide the ability to highlight, tag, and share favorite parts; access links to games, websites, resources, and information; and connect with other readers.

"Everywhere I have sought rest and not found it, except sitting in a corner by myself with a little book."

—Thomas à Kempis

The good news is that seventy-five percent of kids say that no matter what they can do online, they will always want to be able to read books printed on paper as well. I personally still find it easier to read something on a printed page than on a screen, but there are a number of arguments for reading online. Internet articles, reports, stories, e-books, reviews, letters, even blogs are an important aspect of reading today that some of us from the pre-computer generation may find it difficult to embrace. But this will be the preferred communication method of the future . . . so while I'm not rushing out to buy Amazon's Kindle® just yet, I do think it's important for children to develop the *muscle* of reading online, with the caveat that all the same guidelines about reading for pleasure and empowerment apply—and with that added measure of supervision in terms of Internet safety practices.

Remember that the Internet can be a hugely dangerous place—host to a plethora of addictive games and mindless activities, not mention pornographic and violent content, and populated by predators of all kinds. And while studies show that a *moderate* amount of computer time a week can correlate to improved scores with respect to letter recognition, reading comprehension, etc., more than eight hours a week spent online becomes more problematic than helpful (and has a direct impact on young waistlines, to boot). Most schools and libraries offer Internet safety programs with guidelines and resources, and as parents we should participate in them regularly to stay abreast of the issues.

> *"The reason that fiction is more interesting than any other form of literature, to those who really like to study people, is that in fiction the author can really tell the truth without humiliating himself."*
>
> —Eleanor Roosevelt

Finally, we must be aware of how—and how much—*we* use television and computers ourselves. Even if it's just the news or weather, the distraction of having a TV on in the background will deter any child from getting value out of reading (or any other activity). As parents, we must be mindful of letting the "white noise" of TV, or the addictive nature of email and the Internet, interfere with young imaginations and efforts to concentrate, as well as with our ability to have meaningful and personal interactions with our kids. We must consider what we are modeling when we choose to watch TV or surf the net ourselves as a way to unwind at the end of a long day.

"My son has trouble finding books he likes, and I'm at a loss as how to help. Any suggestions?"

According to a 2008 survey conducted by Scholastic, "trouble finding books they like" is one of the key reasons kids say they don't read more frequently, with boys more likely than girls to have problems in this area. And among parents, almost fifty percent say they have a hard time finding information on books their child would enjoy.

It is for these reasons that I have chosen to include the **"Emma's Family Favorites"** sections at the end of each chapter. You will also find resources for finding great books in the **"Recommended Resources"** section of the book, including dozens of books, publications, organizations, programs, websites, and blogs for connecting parents and children with great books.

The Scholastic survey shows that Moms are the key figures when it comes to elementary school kids getting ideas about which books to read for fun. Middle school kids overwhelmingly rely on their friends and teachers for book recommendations, as do high schoolers (who also rely on the Internet.) The study also indicates that kids like to choose their own books—and that eighty

> *"Books had instant replay long before sports."*
>
> — Bert Williams

nine percent of kids cite their favorite books as those they picked out themselves. For this reason, it's important to look for ways to *help kids find books they love*, rather than appearing to make all the choices for them.

Strategies in this regard include:

- ✐ **Regular visits to libraries and bookstores** (with ample time to let kids explore and choose)
- ✐ **Participation in book fairs, book clubs and other book-related programs and events**—whether at school, the library, or bookstores
- ✐ **Adults researching and obtaining recommended books**, and leaving them in places where they can be "discovered" by kids
- ✐ **Visiting kid-friendly Internet sites** such as www.guysread.com and www.bookhooks.com, along with the others listed in the **"Recommended Resources"** section

"My son read all the Harry Potter books, but hasn't found anything else that grabbed him as much since. It's as if, now that the series is over, he's given up reading!"

The power of Potter! First of all, let's be thankful to J.K. Rowling for her incredible contribution to the world of children's books and the degree to which she has motivated kids to read. The statistics regarding *Harry Potter* are pretty remarkable (from Scholastic's "Kids and Family Reading Report"):

- Seventy five percent of kids say reading *Harry Potter*—or having someone read the books to them—has made them interested in reading other books.
- Two thirds of kids say they do better in school since reading *Harry Potter*, and parents agree.
- Boys are as likely as girls to have read *Harry Potter*.
- Ninety percent of *Harry Potter* readers say they will likely re-read *Harry Potter* books.
- *Harry Potter* readers—especially those who have read all seven—are more passionate about reading in general.

But what to read now that the series is over?

For the most part, kids who love *Harry Potter* will respond to other series in the fantasy genre. Here are some suggestions to try:

- *Artemis Fowl* (Eoin Colfer)
- *Books of Ember* (Jeanne DuPrau)
- *The Chronicles of Narnia* (C.S. Lewis)
- *The Chronicles of Prydain* (Lloyd Alexander)
- *The Dark Is Rising* (Susan Cooper)
- *His Dark Materials* (Philip Pullman)
- *The Lord of the Rings Trilogy* and *The Hobbit* (J.R.R. Tolkien)
- *The Inheritance Series* (Christopher Paolini)
- *Redwall* (Brian Jacques)
- *A Series of Unfortunate Events* (Lemony Snicket)
- *Septimus Heap* (Angie Sage)
- *The Twilight Saga* (Stephenie Meyer)
- *Warriors* (Erin Hunter)
- *The Wednesday Tales* (Jon Berkeley)
- *The Wolves Chronicles* (Joan Aiken)
- *A Wrinkle in Time* (Madeleine L'Engle)

"Your suggestions make sense, but it seems like a lot of work . . . and parenting is challenging (and exhausting!) enough as it is. Will it really make a difference? Is it worth the effort?"

Will employing these techniques make a difference? Without question. As the saying goes, "You catch more flies with honey than with vinegar." There is no greater motivator in life than pleasure . . . and by working to build and sustain the connection between any desired activity and pleasure, you *dramatically* improve your child's chances of pursuing that activity on a regular basis.

Frankly, I extend this philosophy to a lot of other areas of life. Sam is a passionate musician—largely because the focus of his learning and playing (thanks to a great, like-minded teacher) has been on having fun, and playing what he *loves*: classic rock. Instead of drills and rote learning and rigidly imposed practice time, for instance, he has learned skills and theory from listening to, talking about, studying, and playing Dylan and Clapton and the Beatles. We've provided consistent access to good music, quality instruments, fun musical gadgetry, shared dialogue, and, most importantly, a great teacher—and his joy in the discovery has done the rest.

> "When the Day of Judgment dawns and the great conquerors and lawyers and statesmen come to receive their rewards—their crowns, their laurels, their names carved indelibly on imperishable marble—the almighty will turn to Peter and will say, not without a certain envy when he sees us coming with our books under our arms, "Look, these need no reward. We have nothing to give them here. They have loved reading."
>
> —Virginia Woolf

Keep the word *joy* uppermost in your mind at all times. Continue to ask yourself, "Will this lead to *enjoyment* for my child? Will this motivate him or her to want *more*?" and watch what unfolds.

One last note: "Children's books today are so well-written that they are fun even for adults," says the Family Reading Partnership. Chances are these strategies will not only brighten your child's life, but yours as well. You may well be surprised by how much you enjoy putting them to work for you.

Will it be worth it?

Consider these twenty-five compelling reasons to keep reading, and to raise your children to be readers as well:

Readers are more likely to ...

1. Do well in school
2. Communicate effectively
3. Have confidence
4. Be productive
5. Concentrate well
6. Solve problems
7. Seek out and develop new ideas
8. Be lifelong learners
9. Utilize technology
10. Get ahead in their chosen career
11. Earn a higher salary
12. Get a promotion or a raise
13. Cope well with life's challenges
14. Know how to relax and unwind
15. Be creative
16. Be well-rounded
17. Attend cultural events
18. Volunteer or do charity work
19. Be better conversationalists
20. Achieve rewarding relationships
21. Find common humanity
22. Be thoughtful, engaged citizens
23. Vote
24. Live longer, healthier lives
25. Be happy

Convinced? Let's get started!

7

Recommended Resources

"Even if the pleasure of reading has been lost, it hasn't gone very far. It's just under the surface. Easily found. We simply need to know where to look."

—Daniel Pennac, author & educator,
Better Than Life

How to Find Great, Age-Appropriate Books

- Ask your **local librarian, bookseller,** or **preschool teacher** for recommendations.
- Ask the **parents** of children who enjoy reading—and the **children** themselves—for recommendations.
- Check out **bestseller lists**—www.nytimes.com and www.amazon.com both list weekly children's book best sellers
- Explore **award winners**—See the **"Book Awards"** information later in this section to learn more about the notable awards for children's books.
- Pick up the latest editions of the books and magazines listed under **"Books"** and **"Publications"** later in this section.
- Familiarize yourself with the many reading support and literacy **"Organizations and Programs"** and investigate their programs, services, and activities.
- Visit the recommended **"Websites, Blogs, and Other Web Resources"** for countless frequently updated recommendations and resources for finding great children's books.

∾ Comb through Amazon.com and Barnes&Noble.com's lists—
"Listmania" and "Hot Releases" on **Amazon**; "Noteworthy
Children's Books" and "The Picture Book Nook" on the
B&NJr. section of **Barnes&Noble.com**. **Borders** provides similar
lists (www.borders.com). All three sites also offer customer
reviews, discussions, and forums, as well as myriad ways to
search topics, age ranges, etc.

Book Awards

A number of awards are given annually to young people's books for
outstanding writing and illustration. These awards can often be helpful in choosing great books for chil-
dren. Bear in mind, however, that a
number of equally wonderful books
are overlooked by awards commit-
tees or do not receive awards—and
of course, since awards are generally
given by *adult* committee members,
with varying guidelines, opinions,
and mandates to follow, they can't necessarily guarantee that your
child will love a particular book . . .

*"Books are the bees which
carry the quickening pollen
from one to another mind."*

—James Russell Lowell

That said, here are some of the main ones to look out for:

∾ **The American Library Association (ALA)**. Through its Association
of Library Services for Children, ALA gives out a number of
children's book awards, as well as providing "Notable" and
"Best" lists, and offers a complete history of current and past
awards on their website (www.ala.org). Awards usually
include one gold medal and one or more silver or honor book
medals. The main ones include:

  • **The Newbery Medal**—Given annually to an author who has
    written the most distinguished contribution to children's lit-
    erature—usually a novel—published in the United States.

  • **The Caldecott Medal**—Given annually to an illustrator for
    the most distinguished contribution to picture book illus-
    tration in the United States.

  • **The Coretta Scott King Awards**—Given to an African Ameri-
    can author and an African American illustrator whose

books make an outstanding inspirational and educational contribution to children's literature.

- **The Pura Belpré Award**—Given to a Latino/Latina writer and illustrator whose work best portrays, affirms, and celebrates the Latino cultural experience in an outstanding work of literature for children and youth.
- **The Michael L. Printz Award**—Given for excellence in young adult literature.
- **The Odyssey Award**—Given for excellence in audiobooks.
- **Schneider Family Award**—Given for books that deal with people with disabilities.
- **The Robert F. Sibert Informational Book Award**—Awarded annually to the author(s) and illustrator(s) of the most distinguished informational book.
- **The Theodor Seuss Geisel Award**—Given for the most distinguished American book for beginning readers.

- **Bank Street Children's Book Awards**—Given to a book or books of outstanding literary merit in which young people deal in a positive and realistic way with difficulties in their world and grow emotionally and morally. www.bnkst.edu/bookcom/awards.html

- **Bergh Award**—Awarded by the ASPCA for humane topics in various categories.

- **Boston Globe–Horn Book Awards**—Given annually for excellence in literature for children and young adults in three categories: Picture Book; Fiction and Poetry; and Nonfiction. Honor Books are also named in each category. www.hbook.com

- **The Golden Kite**—Given to children's book authors and artists by the Society of Children's Book Writers & Illustrators. www.scbwi.org

- **National Book Award for Young People's Literature**—Chosen by the National Book Foundation. www.nationalbook.org

- **Orbis Pictus Award**—Given by the NCTE (National Council of Teachers of English) for outstanding nonfiction for children. www.ncte.org

Books

Best Books for Kids Who (Think They) Hate to Read: 125 Books That Will Turn Any Child into a Lifelong Reader (Laura Backes)

Better Than Life (Daniel Pennac)

The Between the Lions Book for Parents: Everything You Need to Know to Help Your Child Learn to Read (Linda K. Rath, Louise Kennedy)

Books Kids Will Sit Still For (Judy Freeman)

Great Books About Things Kids Love (Kathleen Odean)

> *Great Books for Boys*
>
> *Great Books for Girls*

Guys Write for Guys Read (Jon Scieszka)

Honey for a Child's Heart: The Imaginative Use of Books in Family Life (Gladys Hunt)

How to Get Your Child to Love Reading (Esmé Raji Codell)

The Book of Junior Authors and Illustrators **series** (edited by Connie Rockman, 8th, 9th and 10th editions)

> *"Books are uniquely portable magic."*
>
> —Stephen King

The Kids' Book Club Book: Reading Ideas, Recipes, Activities, and Smart Tips for Organizing Terrific Kids' Book Clubs (Judy Gelman, Vicki Levy Krupp)

The Mother-Daughter Book Club: How Ten Busy Mothers and Daughters Came Together to Talk, Laugh, and Learn Through Their Love of Reading (Shireen Dodson)

The New York Times Parent's Guide to the Best Books for Children (Eden Ross Lipson)

Reading Magic—Why Reading Aloud to Our Children Will Change Their Lives Forever (Mem Fox)

Read to Me: Raising Kids Who Love to Read (Bernice E. Cullinan)

The Read-Aloud Handbook (Jim Trelease)

Under the Chinaberry Tree: Books and Inspirations for Mindful Parenting (Ann Ruethling and Patti Pitcher)

Valerie and Walter's Best Books for Children—A Lively, Opinionated Guide (Valerie Lewis and Walter M. Mayes)

Magazines, Journals, and Other Publications

American Libraries **magazine**—Published 10 times a year by the American Library Association (ALA). www.ala.org/ala/alonline/index.cfm

The Best Children's Books of the Year, published annually by the Children's Book Committee of the Bank Street College of Education. www.bankstreetbooks.com

Book Links—Published by ALA for teachers, librarians, library media specialists, booksellers, parents, and other adults interested in connecting children with high-quality books. www.ala.org/ala/productsandpublications/periodicals/booklinks/booklinks.cfm

Booklist—ALA's weekly subscription magazine, delivering over 8,000 recommended-only reviews of books, audiobooks, reference sources, video, and DVD titles each year. Full coverage of ALA award winners, as well as the annual Editor's Choice and Top of the List issues, ALA Notables, and other "best" lists. With interviews, essays, and columns, this is a wealth of useful information and lively discussion. www.booklistonline.com

Chinaberry—Excellent catalog committed to recommending wonderful, uplifting books that color life in a positive way, and to helping children grow into caring, gentle adults. www.chinaberry.com

The Horn Book Magazine and *The Horn Book Guide*—Distinguished journals in the field of children's and young adult literature. www.hbook.com

Publishers Weekly—Weekly magazine for all the news of the publishing industry. Also offers the weekly *Children's Bookshelf* newsletter online. www.publishersweekly.com

Reading Today—the bimonthly newspaper of the International Reading Association (IRA), with news about literacy education, trends, strategies, and advocacy. www.reading.org/publications/reading_today/index.html

Organizations and Programs

There are hundreds of local, national, and international organizations that promote literacy and provide programs to support reading, writing, and the role of books in children's lives. The following is a selection of some of the most prominent. A comprehensive list can be found at the **Library of Congress's "Center for the Book"** site: www.loc.gov/loc/cfbook/partners/.

American Library Association (ALA)—The oldest and largest library association in the world, with a mission to promote the highest quality library and information services and public access to information. ALA offers professional services and publications to members and nonmembers, including many industry and consumer magazines on the topics of reading, library services, and publishing (see the **"Magazines, Journals, and Other Publications"** section). It also provides distinguished annual awards to authors and illustrators (see the **"Book Awards"** section) as well as important annual lists, such as Notable Children's Books, Best Books for Young Adults, Notable Children's Recordings, and Selected Audiobooks for Young Adults. ALA also provides tools for literacy and advocacy, reference sources, and much more. www.ala.org

> *"Story is an innate paradigm for enjoying and understanding life."*
>
> —Philip Pullman, author

Bank Street Books—New York's best bookstore for and about children, affiliated with the Bank Street College of Education, whose Children's Book Committee produces the annual publication *The Best Children's Books of the Year*, and offers several awards for excellence in children's literature. www.bankstreetbooks.com

The Center for the Book, Library of Congress—A partnership between government and the private sector, dedicated to using the resources and prestige of the Library of Congress to stimulate public interest in books and reading, to support literacy and library promotion, and to encourage the historical study of books, reading, and the printed word. The center's website is a unique resource directory with links to more than 250 organizations that promote books, reading, literacy, and libraries, as well as information about forthcoming events, a list of the center's publications, and other projects—including

Letters About Literature, River of Words, the National Ambassador for Young People's Literature, the National Book Festival, One Book community reading projects (including **Big Read**)—and literary events taking place across the country. www.loc.gov/loc/cfbook

The Children's Book Council (CBC)—the nonprofit trade association of publishers and packagers of books and related materials for children and young adults. The goals of the CBC are:

- ✍ To make the reading and enjoyment of children's books an essential part of America's educational and social goals

- ✍ To enhance public perception of the importance of reading by disseminating information about books and related materials for young people and information about children's book publishing, and

- ✍ To create materials to support literacy and reading encouragement programs (such as newsletters, magazines, and reading lists) and to encourage the annual observance of **National Children's Book Week** and **Young People's Poetry Week**. www.cbcbooks.org

Family Reading Partnership—A non-profit coalition of individuals, businesses, schools, libraries, and other organizations who join forces to "create a culture of literacy" by promoting family reading practices and creating programs that provide books and encouragement for families to make reading aloud to their children a part of everyday life. www.familyreading.org

First Book—A non-profit organization that gives children from low-income families the opportunity to read and own their first new books. www.firstbook.org

IndieBound—The independent bookseller's network; a local and national effort to shine a light on the knowledge and diversity of independent bookstores, via the Indie Next List, an eclectic monthly selection of new books chosen by independent booksellers. www.indiebound.org/indie-next-list

International Reading Association (IRA)—The non-profit, international membership organization for literacy professionals and reading teachers, providing advocacy, global outreach, awards and grants, conferences, and numerous publications, including peer-reviewed journals and the bimonthly newspaper *Reading Today*. www.reading.org

Jumpstart—A program to build literacy, language, social, and initiative skills in young children by pairing motivated college students with preschoolers in caring and supportive one-to-one relationships for an entire school year. www.jstart.org

National Book Foundation—Home of the National Book Awards and multiple programs celebrating the best of American literature. www.nationalbook.org

The National Children's Book and Literacy Alliance—A not-for-profit organization founded by award-winning young people's authors and illustrators with the goal of keeping young people's literacy, literature, and libraries an ongoing priority on the national agenda. www.thencbla.org

National Council of Teachers of English (NCTE)—Advancing teaching, research, and student achievement in English language arts at all scholastic levels, and offering a range of special programs to reach out to underserved communities, celebrate multicultural literature, advance knowledge about critical education issues, better prepare teachers for success in the classroom, and safeguard intellectual freedom. www.ncte.org

National Institute for Literacy—A federal agency providing leadership on literacy issues. Working in consultation with the U.S. Departments of Education, Labor, and Health and Human Services, the Institute serves as a national resource on current, comprehensive literacy research, practice, and policy. Programs include the National Early Literacy Panel, the Commission on Reading Research, and evaluation of reading assessment programs, as well as providing ongoing national statistics on the state of reading in America. www.nifl.gov

> *"For this reconciliation [with reading] to take place: we must ask for nothing in return. Ask not a single question. Do not assign the smallest scrap of homework. Reading is a gift. Read, and wait. Read and trust the eyes that open slowly, the faces that light up, the questions that will begin to form and give way to other questions."*
>
> —Daniel Pennac,
> *Better Than Life*

Reach Out and Read—A non-profit organization that provides new books for children and offers advice to parents about the importance of reading aloud via pediatricians' offices and exam rooms across the nation. www.reachoutandread.org

Reading Is Fundamental (RIF)—The oldest and largest children's and family nonprofit literacy organization in the United States, dedicated to preparing and motivating children to read by delivering free books and literacy resources to those children and families who need them most. Among other programs, RIF sponsors community volunteers in every state and provides 4.5 million children a year with 16 million new, free books through their **Books for Ownership** program, helps parents develop the skills to take a leading role in supporting their children's reading and learning through their **Family of Readers** and **Shared Beginnings** programs, and promotes reading at the 1st grade level with the Running Start challenge. www.rif.org

"Some people will lie, cheat, steal and back-stab to get ahead . . . and to think, all they have to do is READ."

—Fortune Magazine

Reading Rockets—A national multimedia project offering information and resources on how young kids learn to read, why so many struggle, and how caring adults can help. The Reading Rockets project is comprised of PBS television programs, online services, and resources providing news headlines, research-based articles, tips for parents and educators, video interviews with top children's book authors, a monthly e-newsletter, blogs by leading industry specialists, national and local resources, and an online store, as well as teleconferences and free webcasts for teacher professional development. www.readingrockets.org

Target—The Target Corporation is an extraordinary example and resource when it comes to literacy advocacy. As part of their education-based community outreach, Target sponsors a host of reading-related events, programs, and activities, including:

> **Book Festivals**—Free festivals around the country, which include author and illustrator appearances, costumed characters from kids' favorite books and storytelling stages for the whole family.

Family Reading Night —Target-sponsored events held at local schools, featuring guest readers, educational and fun activities, and book swaps. Get a free planning kit at www.schoolfamilynights.com.

Letters about Literature—A national reading-writing contest for grades 4–12, held in partnership with **The Center for the Book at the Library of Congress**, in which readers write a personal letter to an author, living or dead, from any genre explaining how that author's work changed the student's thinking. http://www.loc.gov/loc/cfbook/letters/

Ready. Sit. Read!—Providing resources, tips, and activities to support reading.

Target also maintains partnerships with:

Reach Out and Read—A national non-profit organization that promotes early literacy by giving new books to children and advice to parents about the importance of reading aloud in pediatric exam rooms across the nation. www.reachoutandread.org

United Through Reading—A national organization dedicating to uniting families facing physical separation (especially military families) by facilitating the bonding experience of reading aloud together. www.unitedthroughreading.org

Visit www.target.com and click on "Community" to learn more.

United Nations Educational, Scientific, and Cultural Organization—UNESCO's literacy portal is dedicated to keeping literacy high on national, regional, and international agendas. www.unesco.org/education/literacy

Websites, Blogs and Other Web Resources

www.thebestkidsbooksite.com—"An Interactive Media Channel where Books, Crafts, Podcasts, Online Video and Web Resources Intersect."

Between the Lions—The website of PBS's *Between the Lions* TV show, celebrating libraries and literacy. A wealth of resources—activities, quick tips, recommended books and curriculum materials—for parents and educators. http://pbskids.org/lions/

Bookhooks—"The world's best book reporting site," featuring illustrated book reports posted by kids. www.bookhooks.com

Children's Choices—Thousands of students and teachers vote on annual favorites. www.reading.org/resources/tools/choices.html

The Children's Literature Web Guide—Links to the growing number of Internet resources related to books for children and young adults. www.ucalgary.ca/~dkBrown/index.html

Cynsations—The blog of Cynthia Leitich Smith, YA author and faculty member at the Vermont College of Fine Arts, MFA program in Writing for Children and Young Adults. Features interviews, reading recommendations, publishing information, literacy advocacy, writer resources, and news in children's and young adult literature. http://cynthialeitichsmith.blogspot.com

A Fuse #8 Production—The blog of Elizabeth (Betsy) Bird, a children's librarian with the New York Public Library, featuring reviews of new children's books and links to what's happening in the field. www.schoollibraryjournal.com/blog/1790000379.html

www.guysread.com—Author/illustrator and 2008 National Ambassador for Young People's Literature Jon Scieszka's website, motivating boys to read by connecting them with materials they will want to read, in ways they like to read.

International Children's Digital Library—Offers a wide spectrum of children's books, available for free in more than 44 languages. Students are invited to share reviews of the books they have read. www.icdlbooks.org

www.judyreadsbooks.com—The website of Judy Freeman, children's literature specialist and author of *Books Kids Will Sit Still For*.

Kidsbookshelf—Book reviews and more. www.kidsbookshelf.com

Light Up Your Brain and Sound Stories—Downloadable audio versions of popular fairy tales and storybooks. Available as MP3 files, these stories can be enjoyed in the classroom listening center, car, or family room. http://lightupyourbrain.com/audio-stories-for-children.html

Literacy Connections—Promoting literacy and a love of reading by providing a wealth of information on, articles about, and links to reading and teaching techniques as well as literacy resources and programs. http://literacyconnections.com/

Lookybook—Allows you to look at picture books in their entirety—from cover to cover, at your own pace, before you buy. www.lookybook.com

NoveList—An online database of over 155,000 fiction titles, and a wide range of support content, available for free through most public libraries. www.ebscohost.com/thisTopic.php?topicID=16&marketID=6

Planet Esmé—The website of author and "certified readiologist" Esmé Raji Codell. Also check out her blog, which features "The PlanetEsme Book-A-Day Plan: The Best New Children's Books from Esmé's Shelf." www.planetesme.com and planetesme.blogspot.com

> *"Wear the old coat and buy the new book."*
>
> —Austin Phelps

Reading Rockets' "Blogs About Reading"—Weekly insight into the best practices in reading instruction and using books effectively from leading specialists in the field. www.readingrockets.org/blogs

Read Kiddo Read—James Patterson's new website recommending great books for kids. www.readkiddoread.com

www.ReadWriteThink.org—A partnership between the International Reading Association (IRA), the National Council of Teachers of English (NCTE), and the Verizon Foundation, providing web resources, online fun, and learning beyond the classroom.

Starfall—A free online program containing a series of animated interactive storybooks at beginning, intermediate, and advanced reading levels. Emergent and early reader books highlight individual letters, vowel sounds, and letter combinations. If a reader does not recognize a word in the text, he or she can place the cursor on it and receive visual and voice assistance. As the reading level increases, so do the reading choices, including a variety of myths, fables, plays, fiction, and nonfiction texts. www.starfall.com

TumbleBooks—An online library of animated, talking picture books, read-along titles, and streaming audio books. www.Tumblebooks.com

www.walterthegiant.com/book.html—Valerie Lewis and Walter M. Mayes's "Best Books for Children" website.

Appendix

Tables

TABLE 1: *Creating the Connections* – Strategies for Each Age Group

Subheading	Page	Babies & Toddlers	Pre-schoolers	Elementary school	Middle school and beyond
Overarching Strategies					
Read together	16	✔	✔	✔	✔
Set a good example	17	✔	✔	✔	✔
In the Home					
Warm, inviting atmosphere	17	✔	✔	✔	✔
Cuddle while reading	17	✔	✔	✔	✔
Offer a toy or snack	17	✔	✔		
Regular "reading time"	18	✔	✔	✔	
Create/maintain a ritual	18	✔	✔	✔	
Return to favorites	18	✔	✔	✔	
Fridge/tub letters and spelling games	18	✔	✔	✔	
Books everywhere	19	✔	✔	✔	✔
Timing sensitivity	31		✔	✔	
Book nook	31		✔	✔	✔
Attractive displays	31		✔	✔	
Experimental displays	32		✔	✔	
Book-of-the-Month club	32		✔	✔	✔
Impromptu book gifts	32		✔	✔	✔
Never withhold, or threaten with, books	32		✔	✔	✔
Reading in bed	60			✔	✔
Organized books	93				✔
Beyond the Home					
Visit libraries and bookstores	19	✔	✔	✔	✔
Books as gifts	19	✔	✔	✔	✔
Read on outings	19	✔			
Arts programs	33		✔	✔	✔

TABLE 2: *Actions and Activities* — Strategies for Each Age Group

Subheading	Page	Babies & Toddlers	Pre-schoolers	Elementary school	Middle school and beyond
Overarching Strategy					
Connect reading to life skills	34		✔	✔	✔
Supporting Your Child					
Books as problem solvers	34		✔	✔	✔
Support activities	35		✔	✔	✔
Advocacy at school	36		✔	✔	✔
Familiarity with what they are reading at school	97				✔
Set goals and offer rewards	97				✔
Encouraging Exploration					
Make up your own stories	36		✔	✔	
Kids illustrate	37		✔	✔	
Record yourself reading	37		✔	✔	
Play storytelling games	37		✔	✔	✔
Storytime play date	37		✔	✔	
Write to your kids	37		✔	✔	✔
Explore family history	65			✔	✔
Author study	66			✔	✔
Skill Building					
Tell your childhood stories	38		✔	✔	
Help kids make their own books	38		✔	✔	✔
Play word games	38		✔	✔	✔
Cook together	39		✔	✔	✔
Involve in chores	34		✔	✔	✔
Encourage kids to write their own stories	67			✔	✔
Promote journaling	67			✔	✔
Year-end family newsletter	67			✔	✔
Beyond the Home					
Related movies or plays	39		✔	✔	✔
Audiobooks	40		✔	✔	✔
Join or start a book club	69			✔	✔
Start a collection	69			✔	✔
Armchair travel	69			✔	✔
Time capsule	71			✔	✔
Journalistic activities	102				✔
Online book reviews	102				✔
Altruism	102				✔

TABLE 3: *What to Read* — Recommendations for Each Age Group

Subheading	Page	Babies & Toddlers	Pre-schoolers	Elementary school	Middle school and beyond
Soft books	19	✔			
Books about babies/familiar things	20	✔			
Few words or pics per page	20	✔			
Simple plots; few sentences per page	41		✔		
Fairy/folk tales	41		✔	✔	
Animal tales	20	✔	✔	✔	
Poetry	20	✔	✔	✔	✔
Interactive (flaps, textures, etc.)	21	✔	✔		
Homemade photo books	21	✔	✔		
Counting / ABC's	21	✔	✔		
Beyond books: magazines, etc.	23	✔	✔	✔	✔
Fuel child's passions/interests	41		✔	✔	✔
Reference books	42		✔	✔	✔
Science books	42		✔	✔	✔
Wordless books	42		✔		
Longer picture books/Chapter books	43		✔	✔	
Book/toy packages	43		✔	✔	
TV tie-ins	43		✔	✔	
Books about same-age kids and relevant experiences	75				
Series books	75			✔	✔
How-to books	76			✔	✔
Comic books/graphic novels	76			✔	✔
Riddle books	104				✔
Puberty books	105				✔
Books by kids	105				✔
Chapter books and novels	105				✔
Historical fiction	105				✔
Biographies and/or autobiographies	105				✔
Survival stories	105				✔
Motivational books	105				✔
The classics	106				✔

TABLE 4: *Reading Techniques* — Strategies for Each Age Group

Subheading	Page	Babies & Toddlers	Pre-schoolers	Elementary school	Middle school and beyond
Overarching Strategies					
Invite participation	22	✔	✔	✔	✔
Enlist others to read	22	✔	✔	✔	✔
Provide practical connections	46		✔	✔	
Developing Listening and Thinking Skills					
Offer snack or toy	46		✔		
Stop to ask questions	46		✔	✔	✔
Relate to previous books	78			✔	✔
Follow up on a story	78			✔	✔
Read-Aloud Skills					
Read with a colorful voice	22	✔	✔	✔	✔
Point to things	22	✔	✔		
Monitor interest level	22	✔	✔		
Introduce the book before you begin	46		✔	✔	✔
Trace lines with finger	46		✔		
Slow down	46		✔	✔	✔
End sentences with periods	47		✔	✔	✔
Maximizing Interest					
Use character voices or accents	48		✔	✔	✔
Personalize the story	48		✔		
Role play with dialogue	79			✔	
Stop at suspense points	79			✔	✔

Bibliography

"2008 Kids and Family Reading Report." New York: Scholastic, 2008. www.scholastic.com/readingreport.

American Library Association. www.ala.org.

Center for the Book, Library of Congress. www.loc.gov/loc/cfbook.

Children's Book Council. www.cbcbooks.org.

Codell, Esmé R. *How to Get Your Child to Love Reading*. Chapel Hill: Algonquin, 2003.

Crain, Caleb. "Twilight of the Books." *The New Yorker*, 24 Dec. 2007.

Cullinan, Bernice E. *Read to Me: Raising Kids Who Love to Read*. New York: Scholastic, 2006.

Family Reading Partnership. www.familyreading.org.

"Fast Facts on Literacy." Humboldt Literacy Project/National Institute of Literacy. 2001. www.eurekawebs.com/humlit/fast_facts.htm.

Feinberg, Barbara. "Reflections on the 'Problem Novel.'" *American Educator* (2004). www.aft.org/pubs-reports/american_educator/issues/winter04-05/problemnovel.htm

Fox, Mem. *Reading Magic: Why Reading Aloud to Our Children Will Change Their Lives Forever*. New York: Harvest Books, 2008.

Gore, Al. *The Assault on Reason*. New York: Penguin, 2007. 6–20.

Grabois, Andrew. "The Flip Side." *Beneath the Cover*. 10 Dec. 2007. www.beneaththecover.com.

Grabois, Andrew. "The Sad State of Reading in America—Even for Adults." *Beneath the Cover*. 03 Dec. 2007. www.beneaththecover.com.

Hunt, Gladys. *Honey for a Child's Heart*. Grand Rapids, MI: Zondervan, 2002.

"Illiteracy: a National Crisis. United Way's Role." Report From United Way of America's Strategic Planning Committee, 1987.

International Reading Association. www.reading.org.

Jenkins, Jerold. Jenkins Group Inc., Book Publishing. www.bookpublishing.com.

Kozol, Jonathan. *Illiterate America*. New York: Plume, 1986.

LeGuin, Ursula K. "Staying Awake: Notes on the Alleged Decline of Reading." *Harper's*. Feb. 2008: 33–38.

Literacy Connections. http://literacyconnections.com.

National Adult Literacy Survey. (1001) U.S. Department of Education.

National Center for Education Statistics. IES/NCES. U.S. Department of Education and the Institute of Education Sciences. http://nces.ed.gov/.

"National Endowment for the Arts Announces New Reading Study." National Endowment for the Arts. 19 Nov. 2007. www.nea.gov/news/news07/TRNR.html.

National Institute for Literacy. www.nifl.gov.

"Parents." Reading is Fundamental. www.rif.org/parents/.

Pennac, Daniel. *Better Than Life*. York, Maine: Stenhouse, 1999.

Poynter, Dan. *Statistics*. ParaPublishing. http://bookstatistics.com.

Publishers Weekly. www.publishersweekly.com.

"Reading At Risk." National Endowment for the Arts. 2004. http://www.nea.gov/pub/readingatrisk.pdf.

"Reading Quotes." www.richmond.k12.va.us/readamillion/readingquotes.htm.

"Reading Quotes." The Literacy Company. www.readfaster.com.

Reading Rockets. www.readingrockets.org.

Rich, Motoko. "A Good Mystery: Why We Read." *The New York Times* 25 Nov. 2007, sec. Week in Review. www.nytimes.com.

Rich, Motoko. "Study Links Drop in Test Scores to a Decline in Time Spent Reading." *The New York Times* 19 Nov. 2007, sec. Arts. www.nytimes.com

Sara, Gail. Reading Lady. www.readinglady.com.

Standards for the English Language Arts. National Council on Teachers of English (NCTE).

Toppo, Greg. "Interview with Author Jon Scieszka." *USA Today* 3 Feb. 2008, sec. News: Education.

Trelease, Jim. *The Read-Aloud Handbook*. New York, NY: Penguin, 2006.

Winerip, Michael. "Mission: Making a Love of Reading Happen." *The New York Times* 14 Oct. 2007, sec. In the Region. www.newyorktimes.com

Index

About the Author

"Books are the quietest and most constant of friends; they are the most accessible and wisest of counselors, and the most patient of teachers."

—**Charles W. Eliot**, *The Happy Life*

EMMA WALTON HAMILTON is a best-selling children's book author, professional editor, and arts educator. In 1992, Emma co-founded the Bay Street Theatre in Sag Harbor, New York, and until 2008 served as the Theatre's Director of Education and Programming for Young Audiences. She continues to act as Education Consultant for the theatre. Emma is also the Editorial Director for The Julie Andrews Collection publishing program (www.julie andrewscollection.com), dedicated to providing quality books for young readers that nurture the imagination and celebrate a sense of wonder, and works as a freelance editor for children's books.

Together with her mother, Julie Andrews, Emma has co-authored seventeen children's books, including the *Dumpy the Dump Truck* series of picture books, board books, and Early Readers (illustrated by her father, Tony Walton), the original fable and national best-seller *Simeon's Gift*, the medieval novel *Dragon: Hound of Honor*, the best-selling middle grade novel about Broadway mice, *The Great American Mousical*, and *Thanks to You—Wisdom from Mother and Child*, a #1 New York Times Bestseller.

Recently, Emma and her mother completed the libretto for the stage adaptation of *Simeon's Gift*, which was produced at Bay Street Theatre in the fall of 2007 and as a national symphonic tour in 2008. Emma has also co-written lyrics for several songs, including "The Show Must Go On," recorded by Julie Andrews, and "On My Way," recorded by Laughing Pizza, www.laughingpizza.com.

A former actress, Emma worked in theater, film and television for ten years before turning her attention towards directing, producing, writing, and educating. She was a faculty member at the Ensemble Studio Theatre Institute in New York City, then served as Bay Street Theatre's Co-Artistic Director for thirteen years, at which point she chose to focus on creating and managing the Theatre's educational and young audience programs. In addition to the Young Playwrights Program (the flagship of Bay Street's educational outreach), Emma administered Bay Street's Internship Program for serious students of technical theatre and the Continuing Classes courses for adults and children in acting, singing, and playwriting. She was also responsible for creating, booking, and managing Kidstreet, the Theatre's highly acclaimed, year-round variety performance series for young audiences.

Emma is a member of the Authors Guild, the Dramatists Guild, The Society of Children's Book Writers and Illustrators, the International Reading Association, Editorial Freelancer's Association, SAG, AEA, AFTRA, and ASCAP. She has served on the theater panel for the New York State Council on the Arts, as an ambassador for the Broadway League's "Kids Night on Broadway," and as a trustee for the former Morriss Center School in Bridgehampton, NY. She lives in Sag Harbor, NY, with her husband, producer/actor Stephen Hamilton, and their two children, Sam and Hope—all of whom love to read.

For more information, visit www.emmawaltonhamilton.com.

Other Books by Emma Walton Hamilton

Published by Hyperion Books for Children

Dumpy the Dump Truck (co-authored with Julie Andrews, illustrated by Tony Walton)

Dumpy at School

Dumpy and the Big Storm

Dumpy Saves Christmas

Dumpy's Friends on the Farm

Dumpy and His Pals

Published by Harper Collins

Dumpy and the Firefighters (co-authored with Julie Andrews, illustrated by Tony Walton)

Dumpy's Happy Holiday

Dumpy's Extra Busy Day

Dumpy's Apple Shop

Dumpy's Valentine

Dumpy to the Rescue!

Simeon's Gift (co-authored with Julie Andrews, illustrated by Gennady Spirin)

Thanks to You: Wisdom from Mother and Child (co-authored with Julie Andrews)

The Great American Mousical (co-authored with Julie Andrews, illustrated by Tony Walton)

Dragon: Hound of Honor (co-authored with Julie Andrews)

Published by Little, Brown Books for Children:

Julie Andrews' Collection of Favorite Poems, Songs and Lullabies (co-authored with Julie Andrews, illustrated by James McMullan, Fall 2009)

The Very Fairy Princess (co-authored with Julie Andrews, Spring 2010)

OTHER BOOKS IN THE JULIE ANDREWS COLLECTION

Published by HarperCollins Publishers; edited by Emma Walton Hamilton.

Picture Books

Grateful: A Song of Giving Thanks (John Bucchino/Anna-Liisa Hakkarainen)

Little Kisses (Jolie Jones/Julie Downing)

Pebble: A Story About Belonging (Susan Milord)

Holly Claus: The Christmas Princess (Brittney Ryan/Laurel Long)

Chapter Books

Mandy (Julie Andrews Edwards)

The Last of the Really Great Whangdoodles (Julie Andrews Edwards)

The Legend of Holly Claus (Brittney Ryan)

Blue Wolf (Catherine Creedon)

The Little Grey Men (B.B.)

The Palace of Laughter, The Tiger's Egg, and *The Lightning Key* (Jon Berkeley)

For updates to the resources, reading lists, and recommendations in this book, visit www.raisingbookworms.com.

We'd like to hear from you for subsequent editions of this book!

Please email your recommendations and success stories with respect to helping children love reading at mail@beechtreebooks.com.